WRESTLING

THE OFFICIAL BOOK

WORLD WRESTLING FEDERATION ®

WRESTLING

THE OFFICIAL BOOK

MALLARD
PRESS

Mallard Press
An imprint of BDD Promotional Book Company, Inc.
666 Fifth Avenue
New York, N.Y. 10103

Mallard Press and the accompanying duck logo are
registered trademarks of the BDD Promotional Book
Company, Inc. Registered in the US Patent and
Trademark Office.

First published in the United States of America in
1992 by the Mallard Press.

Copyright © 1992 TitanSports, Inc.
Design © 1992 Reed International Books Limited

All rights reserved.

Printed and bound in China
D.T.P. Design: Tony Truscott Designs

For copyright reasons this edition may not be sold
outside the United States of America

ISBN 0-792-45803-6

Author: Edward R. Ricciuti

Photographs by Stephen H. Taylor, Photography
Director, TitanSports, Inc., and Tom Buchanan, Staff
Photographer, TitanSports, Inc., except the
photographs from the films *No Holds Barred* and
Suburban Commando which are reproduced courtesy
of New Line Cinema

Portions of this book were written by Keith Elliot
Greenberg, Field Editor, WWF Magazine

Special thanks to: Midge Bacon, Copy Editor,
TitanSports Publications; Felicia Beech, Licensing
Coordinator, Titan Sports, Inc.; Tricia Breheney,
Publisher's Assistant, TitanSports Publications;
Thomas H.W. Emanuel, Publisher and Editor-in-
Chief, TitanSports Publications; Michael Feinberg,
Broadcast Creative Director, TitanSports, Inc.; Amy
Prior, Assistant to the Broadcast Creative Director,
TitanSports, Inc.; and Quinn Tinkoff, Photo Editor,
TitanSports Publications.

CONTENTS

Introduction by
HULK HOGAN

When I was asked to write the introduction to the official book of the WWF, I thought about it for a long while. Hulkamaniacs, I wanted to say something really profound, brother. The WWF has caused some real changes in the world. It's brought people, like my Hulkamaniacs, together. I think of Hulkamaniacs and their families, all gathered around, watching *WrestleMania* on television or going to the arena and seeing the best athletes I've ever known go all out in the squared circle. In that ring, all kinds of rights and wrongs have been sorted out. The Hulkster can tell you that's a fact, because he's been there. And he's still there. After I thought for a long time, I said to myself, "Hulkster, just write what you think." So, Hulkamaniacs, here it is. This book brings you inside the WWF. It gives you a total and thorough look at what's happened — and what's happening. It's the only official WWF publication that looks at the whole WWF. Want to know about

the key matches of *WrestleManias*? It's here. Want to know about the real superstars of the WWF? Turn these pages. The managers? This book tells about them, too. This book also takes you behind the scenes. It gives you a look at WWF publications, television and charity work. Furthermore I'd like to say that many of my colleagues in the WWF spend hours and hours helping other people. You don't always hear about it, but it happens all the time. People like the Big Boss Man and Randy Savage, I'll tell you, they're out there helping other people. All the time. They've made it big in the WWF — and they're spreading it around. I have to admit something. This book tells about other kinds of people in the WWF, people who don't sit right with the Hulkster — like Ric Flair and the Nasty Boys. They're not my kind. What they stand for goes against my grain, brother. But they're great athletes and competitors, even if they take the low road. What you have here in this book is a complete guide to the WWF, a book you can use every time you go to the arena and every time you watch WWF television. It gives you perspective, man, and it gives you an eye to the future. It's a book you can read time and time again and each time learn something new. It's in my library. I hope it's in yours. ■

THE SUPERSTARS OF WWF

They are considered to be among the finest athletes in the world. They include men of superhuman strength, awesome stature, agility that is almost unbelievable and legendary toughness. Some of them are superior role models, altruistic and courageous. Others pride themselves on

unscrupulous behavior, are out totally for themselves and are full of bravado. They are the superstars of the World Wrestling Federation.

The pages that follow contain profiles of the WWF superstars, together with vital statistics and insights into their ambitions and goals.

The profiles make for exciting reading and also provide a comprehensive reference for any fan of the World Wresting Federation. ■

Weight:
303 pounds

From:
Venice Beach, California

Birthday:
August 11

Favorite finishing hold:
Legdrop off the ropes

Trademark:
Unflinching adherence to his values

Favorite quote:
"My strength comes from my Hulkamaniacs."

Goal:
To be remembered as a man who stood by his principles

The time was January 23, 1984. The setting was New York City's Madison Square Garden. A massive young wrestler called Hulk Hogan was belly-down on the mat, his face expressing total agony. Atop his back, cinched in and applying all of his awesome force, the bald-headed Iron Sheik, now known as Colonel Mustafa, applied the dreaded Camel Clutch. The clutch, a reverse chinlock made more agonizing by the Sheik's unique version, was a hold from which no wrestler had ever escaped. It was sure submission — and it had brought the Sheik to the WWF Championship, which Hogan had challenged. The Sheik was ready to claim another victim. But he didn't. Because that night in Madison Square Garden, *Hulkamania* was born.

As Hogan resisted with every ounce of his energy and courage, the fans became one with him. One person, then another and then thousands of others began chanting, "Hogan! Hogan! Hogan!" And Hulk Hogan — who became beloved as the "Hulkster" — felt it. Unbelievably, he struggled to his feet with the Sheik clinging to his back like a demon and broke the feared Camel Clutch. The Sheik was shocked, then shocked again as the Hulkster pounded him to the mat. Then, using a finishing maneuver that is now world famous, Hulk Hogan dropped a big leg on his downed opponent and won the WWF Championship Title.

It was the beginning of a phenomenon that was to rock the world for years. Hulk Hogan had launched himself on a career that would rocket to great heights, making him one of the most well-known and celebrated athletes in the world. And *Hulkamania* would spread to every inhabited continent, uniting millions of people behind the big blond man who would come to stand for the highest of ideals

The Hulkster implores the help of his many Hulkamaniacs during a major match. Go wild, little Hulksters!

. . . .

and who was the epitome of courage. Along the way on his path to greatness, the Hulkster encountered moments of high adventure, eminent satisfaction, pathos, tragedy and rapture. Whether things went for good or ill, he retained his sense of himself and his loyalty to his Hulkamaniacs.

The first major turning point in the Hulkster's career after beating the Sheik was bitter. Andre the Giant, Hogan's fast friend, came under the sway of crafty manager Bobby "The Brain" Heenan and set out to oust the Hulkster from the title. (Andre, of course, long since has changed his ways and again is a stalwart friend of the Hulkster.) At *WrestleMania III*,

> **Eat your vitamins and say your prayers.**
>
> Hulk's advice to youngsters.

Propelled by the Big Boss Man, Hulk gives the boot to Earthquake before Earthquake joined up with Typhoon.

Hogan bodyslammed the Giant and pinned him. The Giant did not learn his lesson. On February 5, 1988, Hogan and Andre met in the squared circle again. Unknown to the Hulkster, a secret deal had been made behind the scenes by Andre, Heenan and the Million Dollar Man Ted DiBiase. A crooked referee, paid off by DiBiase, counted Hogan pinned even though his shoulder was off the mat. Andre, also on the receiving end of DiBiase's dollars, then surrendered the title to the Million Dollar Man.

WWF President Jack Tunney ruled that under WWF regulations the surrender meant the title was vacant and scheduled a tournament at *WrestleMania IV* to decide the new champion. Hogan and Andre were so angry at one another when they met in the tourney that they were disqualified, and eventually Macho Man Randy Savage won the title.

Afterward, Hogan and Savage joined forces as the Mega-Powers. Eventually, the alliance fell apart due to Savage's misplaced envy of the friendship between the Hulkster and Elizabeth. The battle was brutal. Remembers the Macho Man, "I went all out, oh yeaa, I sure did. Lots of times I thought that I had him. But Hulk Hogan doesn't give up. I learned that lesson at *WrestleMania V*. In the end, Hulk was the better man. That time, at least."

THE HULKSTER AND MACHO MAN

Says Hogan of the encounter, "Macho Man Randy Savage is made of steel, man. I hit him with all I had, and he kept coming. But I had an advantage he didn't — *Hulkamania*."

In the end, it was *Hulkamania* that really did inspire Hogan when things looked bleakest. Savage had exploded, ramming the Hulkster's face into a ringpost outside the squared circle and smashing him with a double axhandle off the top turnbuckle. Moments later, with Hogan flat on the mat, Savage scored again from the air, this time with a crunching elbow. But at the eleventh hour, with *Hulkamania* boiling in his veins, the Hulkster arose, booted the Macho Man in the head, then dropped the leg. A three-count later, Hulk Hogan was champion once more.

What was perhaps the epic match thus far in Hogan's career was still to come. It happened at *WrestleMania VI* when the Hulkster met the Ultimate Warrior, then the WWF Intercontinental Champion. It was belt for belt as the two mighty titlists met. Veteran observers say they never have seen two wrestlers push themselves so far beyond the limits of their endurance as did Hogan and the Warrior at Toronto's SkyDome. From the moment they first locked their fingers for an initial test of strength to the finish, when Hogan missed a legdrop and the Warrior big-splashed and pinned him, they never let up. So furious was the confrontation that at one point the referee was caught between the two ring titans and knocked out, failing to see Hogan's obvious pin of the Warrior. Still, to this day, Hogan isn't bitter. "You take things as they come, brother. Those are the breaks. You can't let it get you down."

Hogan didn't. After the Warrior lost the title to Sgt. Slaughter, then under the influence of the evil anti-American General Adnan, Hogan rallied to the flag. Slaughter, Adnan and their confederate, Colonel Mustafa, had reviled the United States and all free nations. At *WrestleMania VII*, Hogan carried his country's banner into the ring against Slaughter and soundly defeated him to gain the title for an unprecedented third time. He would do it a fourth time, as well.

At the 1991 *Survivor Series*, Hogan was challenged for the belt by the Undertaker. By then, Ric Flair, proclaiming himself the "real world's champion," had entered the WWF. He would play a crucial role in Hogan's title reign.

The battle between the Hulkster and the Undertaker was amazing,

Hulk Hogan has also distinguished himself on the motion picture screen, starring in such major films as *No Holds Barred* and *Suburban Commando*.

One of the most difficult times in the Hulkster's life was when Andre the Giant turned on him.

Ric Flair intervened with a ringside chair in a match between Hogan and the Undertaker. The reverberations were felt throughout the WWF when the WWF Title was vacated by WWF President Jack Tunney.

with Hogan somehow surviving the Undertaker's dreaded tombstone reverse piledriver. As the match thundered on, Flair appeared at ringside with a steel chair. Again the Undertaker tried a tombstone. This time, however, Flair inserted the chair, flat on the mat, and Hogan's head hit steel instead of the canvas. He was knocked cold, and the Undertaker became the new champion.

Jack Tunney had seen the chair and ordered a rematch the following Tuesday. Again Flair and a chair would figure in Hogan's destiny. Hogan took the war to the Undertaker and had momentum. But the Hulkster's attention was diverted when

again Flair appeared at ringside, chair in hand. Furious, Hogan went for him. Tunney, watching from ringside, was caught in the fray and knocked cold, as Hogan tangled once more with the Undertaker.

Meanwhile, Flair mounted the ring apron, still with his chair, which he raised in the air. As the Undertaker tried to whip Hogan into it, Hogan reversed, and the WWF's Grim Reaper hit the chair instead. That was all she wrote. The Hulkster reacted quickly and scored the pin. He had become champion for the fourth time.

But the title was not to stay with Hulk. A groggy Tunney remembered seeing Hogan struggling with a chair. He declared the title vacant. The new champion, he said, would be the winner of the 1992 *Royal Rumble*'s 30-man, over-the-top battle royal.

LOOKING TO THE FUTURE

The winner wasn't the Hulkster. Nor was it the Undertaker. It was Ric Flair, who was the third man to enter the ring — wrestlers drew numbers and joined the battle in sequence — and the last to remain. At the end of the battle, Hogan, Flair and Sid Justice were slugging it out. As Hogan strove to oust Flair over the top rope, Justice struck and sent the Hulkster to the concrete. Feeling betrayed, the Hulkster reached up and yanked Justice by the arm as Flair was shoving him from behind. Out went Justice. That left Ric Flair the WWF Champion.

Once again the Hulkster drew a deep breath and went on. He had known defeat before, as he had known victory. He knew that brave men rise from defeat and seek victory once again. The Hulkster took this

knowledge to the ring, toppling one stellar opponent after the other. He seemed to thrive on the adversity that Flair had caused. Deep down, the Hulkster knew that one day he would have the chance to even the score with Ric Flair. So Hogan bided his time and racked up his victories. Would he astonish the world by winning the title for a fifth time? All over the world, fans were betting he would. ■

At the 1992 *Royal Rumble*, the Hulkster fiercely contested Ric Flair. But Sid Justice made the difference.
....

Macho Man Randy Savage

Weight:
245 pounds

From:
Sarasota, Florida

Birthday:
November 15

Favorite finishing hold:
Flying elbow or axhandle off top rope

Trademark:
Total intensity, wild clothes

Favorite quote:
"Oooooh Yeaah!"

Goal:
To be a happily married man forever

Macho Man has been the WWF Intercontinental Champion and, at the *WrestleMania IV* tournament, was crowned the WWF Champion, an event viewed as the pinnacle of his tempestuous career. It wasn't. At *SummerSlam*, in center ring, he married the lovely Elizabeth, who as a manager and friend has stuck with him through thick and thin.

As noted, however, Savage's career has been a wild one. He always has been known as a fiery, if eccentric, individual, a superb athlete who can attack from atop the ropes, grapple on the mat, brawl and execute many technical maneuvers. He is also tough as nails, a quality that has helped him endure against the odds.

Savage's intense and fiery temperament has taken him to many peaks and lows. He has never been one to take the level path. Not Randy Savage. For him, it's the mountaintop or the bottom of a canyon.

There have been several major turning points in Savage's life in and out of the ring, involving either Hulk Hogan or Elizabeth, often both. It was Hogan who helped Savage to the WWF Title at *WrestleMania IV*. Savage and Hogan eventually became fast friends and formed the team known as the "Mega-Powers," with Elizabeth as manager. The Mega-Powers were

Savage executes his spectacular flying elbow off the top turnbuckle.

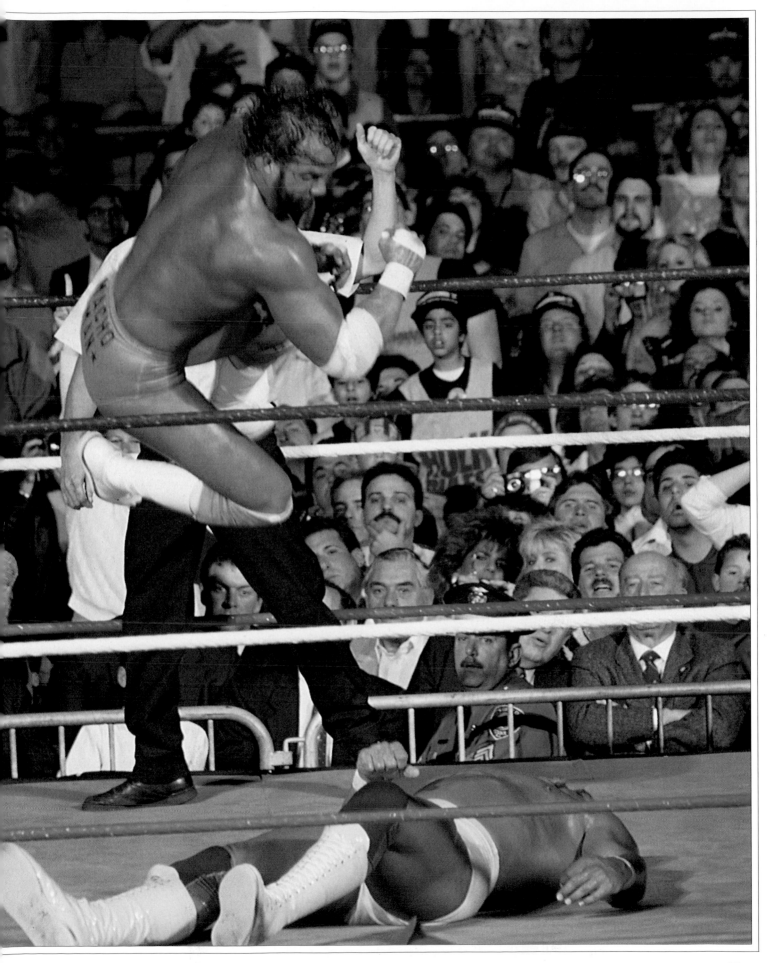

The Macho Man goes after Jake "The Snake" Roberts. Their confrontation was long-lasting and furious before Savage won out. Jake was one of Randy's deadliest enemies.

destroyed when the green monster of jealousy reared its ugly head. Savage became envious over the friendship — and that's all it was — between Elizabeth and the Hulkster. As jealousy mounted, so did his anger toward Hogan. Savage finally attacked the Hulkster in the dressing room after a match with the Twin Towers in which Elizabeth was injured in the melee. Viciously, he cracked the championship belt over Hogan's head and threw Elizabeth down to the floor.

Looking back, Savage expresses remorse for that incident and much that followed. "Oh yeaa," he says. "The Macho Man must have been out of his head to do that to the two people I loved more than anybody else in the world. I was a fool, all screwed up inside my brain. And now I'll admit the Macho Man deserved all he got for what he did."

Savage and Hogan met for the title not long afterward at *WrestleMania V*. The Macho Man was defeated and went on a tear and engaged the witchy Sensational Sherri as his manager. Estranged from Elizabeth and goaded by Sherri, Savage became a vindictive monster, the scourge of the ring. After the Ultimate Warrior won the WWF Title from the Hulkster at *WrestleMania VI*, Sherri pointed Savage toward the new champion. Before

Savage could get his title shot, however, the Warrior took on Sgt. Slaughter. Furious at the Warrior, Savage interfered in the match, knocking the champion unconscious while the referee was distracted. Slaughter had the title, and Savage had a full-blown feud with the Warrior on his hands.

REUNITED WITH ELIZABETH

At *WrestleMania VII*, they met in a match with rules stipulating that the loser must retire. It was a brutal, grueling affair, which the Warrior won after Savage missed an elbowdrop and crashed into the ring barricade. Furious at the loss, Sherri jumped into the ring and began kicking Savage, who was down and out.

Elizabeth had been waiting for a long time, watching Savage's misdeeds and hoping against hope he would change. Unbeknownst to him, she followed his every move. Thus, she was in the audience at *Wrestle Mania VII*. When Sherri attacked Randy, Elizabeth rushed into the ring and drove her out. Savage had lost his career but won an even greater prize. He and Elizabeth were wed.

At the moment of their greatest happiness, however, Savage and Elizabeth were beset by terror, when Jake "The Snake" Roberts and the Undertaker appeared uninvited at the couple's wedding reception. The world was shocked by what happened. The Undertaker pounded Savage, and Jake terrorized Elizabeth with a cobra. For reasons that were known only to Jake, he began a vendetta against the couple, trying to destroy them and their happiness.

Jake had another shock in store. In late 1991, he lured Savage from the WWF television announcer's booth — the Macho Man had become a color commentator — into the ring. After attacking Randy from behind, Jake tied him in the ropes and unleashed the ultimate horror, a king cobra. The serpent bit Savage, sinking its venomous fangs into his arm. Randy might have perished had it not been for swift and proper medical treatment.

"Reinstate me," he pleaded to WWF President Jack Tunney. "Let me face Jake in the ring." After much soul searching, Tunney did reinstate him, and the two met. Savage tore into Roberts and won a surprisingly quick victory. After the match, however, Roberts struck again. He Pearl Harbored Savage, hitting him with skull-crunching DDTs.

With Savage unconscious, Jake produced what looked suspiciously like a snake bag, although Tunney had barred him from bringing reptiles to the ring. When Elizabeth frantically tried to shield Savage, Jake then manhandled her for the world to see. It was an abysmal and horrifying episode, perhaps even more shocking than the fierce assault on Savage by the king cobra.

After that assault, Savage made a vow. "There isn't room enough in the world for me and Jake Roberts. If it's the last thing I do, I will crush that viper's head under my heel. Jake Roberts, you are a doomed man." ∎

The Macho Man exults after reuniting with the lovely Elizabeth at *WrestleMania VII*. At *SummerSlam 1991*, they married.

The Undertaker

Weight:
328 pounds

From:
Death Valley

Birthday:
Unknown

Favorite finishing hold:
Tombstone reverse piledriver

Trademark:
Putting defeated opponents in a body bag

Favorite quote:
"I'll bury you."

Goal:
To put everyone six feet under

The Undertaker reeks of the dank, musty crypt. Around him is the aura of the grave. Managed by the ghoulish Paul Bearer, the Undertaker is in every sense the Grim Reaper of the World Wrestling Federation.

Relentlessly, he stalks his prey in the ring with cold efficiency. Given his immense size, frightening strength and seeming invulnerability to pain, the Undertaker does not need to use complicated ring strategy. He simply over-awes and overpowers the foe. When he wishes, however, the Undertaker can move with astonishing quickness and grace for a man of his bulk. Like a tightrope artist, he can even walk the top rope.

The Undertaker asserts he is in the WWF to exter-minate everyone who stands in his way. Thus, he set out to destroy the symbol of greatness in the WWF, the immortal Hulk Hogan. With the help of another Hogan foe, Ric Flair, the Undertaker assaulted the Hulkster during a television appearance, beating him badly. The Grim Reaper tried to take Hogan's precious cross from around his neck but dropped it to the floor. The cross, it appeared, burned the Undertaker's offending hand.

For a few days after Thanksgiving 1991, it seemed as if the Undertaker had realized his ambition to bury the Hulkster, *Hulkamania* and all the world's loyal Hulkamaniacs. During a title match at the *Survivor Series*, Thanksgiving eve, the Undertaker vanquished Hogan, tombstoning him

He moves with deadly purpose, putting constant pressure on the adversary.

Above: The WWF's Grim Reaper. **Right:** Hulk Hogan is saved by Randy Savage and Rowdy Roddy Piper.

into a chair that had been placed in the ring by Ric Flair.

The match was a wild affair. At first the Undertaker seemed impregnable. Early on, he floored Hogan with a crunching shoulderblock and then began to choke him, trying to squeeze the breath out of him. It was clear that the Undertaker was targeting the Hulkster's throat. Again and again, the Undertaker struck at Hogan's esophagus with brutal punches. When the referee was distracted, the Undertaker's manager, Paul Bearer, also throttled the Hulkster.

A favorite Undertaker tactic is to choke his opponent senseless. Most wrestlers are helpless in the grasp of his lethal strength.

pulverized an ordinary man, but not the Undertaker. Landing like a cat, he hauled Hogan to the arena floor and again went for the throat. Grabbing a microphone cord, the Undertaker wrapped it around the Hulkster's neck and tightened it until Hogan's face turned blue.

BATTLE FOR THE TITLE

Back in the ring, the Undertaker continued to have things all his way. His face utterly devoid of emotion, his eyes unblinking, the Undertaker chopped again at the Hulkster's throat, choked him and then tried to smother him by putting a hand over his mouth. After flattening Hogan with a clothesline, the Undertaker set him up for a tombstone reverse piledriver, which had spelled doom for a long line of Undertaker opponents. Skull-first, the Undertaker drove Hogan into the canvas. To the astonishment of all — even the Undertaker — Hogan sprang to his feet and went at the Undertaker with a vengeance. Just then, Flair appeared at ringside. Hogan took the time to leave the ring and blast him with a right, then turned his attention to the Undertaker once again. It appeared as if Hogan had the match. However, as the Hulkster prepared to bounce off the ropes, Paul Bearer grabbed his legs, and the Undertaker grabbed him for another tombstone. This one worked — but probably only because Flair inserted the chair as Hogan's head came toward the canvas.

Reviewing the match, however, WWF President Jack Tunney ordered a rematch, which was held the following Tuesday. The match seemed to be a repeat of the first as the Undertaker

Eventually, however, the tide turned. Hulk staggered the Undertaker with smashing clotheslines and elbows. Filled with the spirit of *Hulkamania*, the Hulkster tore into his grisly foe with chops and powerful blows to the head and neck. Grabbing the Undertaker, the Hulkster rammed him face-first into the turnbuckles and then put him over the ropes with a clothesline. The blow would have

Once the Undertaker knocks out an opponent, he and manager Paul Bearer waste no time in placing the poor unfortunate in a plastic body bag for the Undertaker to carry away.

choked and shook the Hulkster. Again, Flair appeared with a chair. Hulk went after him, and in the ensuing melee, Tunney, seated at ringside, was knocked cold. As the Undertaker and Hogan resumed their battle, Flair mounted the ring apron, still holding the chair. The Undertaker tried to whip Hulk into it, but Hogan reversed the move and sent the WWF's Grim Reaper into the chair. Moments later, the Hulkster rolled up the Undertaker and pinned him. Hogan had tri-

umphed, taking the title for an unprecedented fourth time. But Tunney, who had revived but was still groggy, had seen the action with the chair. Feeling that the circumstances surrounding the Hulkster's victory were controversial, the WWF president declared the title vacant and up for grabs in the 30-man over-the-top battle royal at the *Royal Rumble.*

People saw another side of the Undertaker, however, when he came to the aid of Macho Man Randy Savage and Elizabeth, saving them from assault by Jake "The Snake" Roberts. It earned the Undertaker Roberts' deep enmity. But the Undertaker fears no one. He already has looked death in the face — and he has laughed at it. ∎

> 66 **Sooner or later, the Undertaker will take all who oppose him into the darkness of the grave. They shall never return to the world of the living.** 99
> **PAUL BEARER**

Ric Flair, a battle-tested veteran of the ring wars, came to the World Wrestling Federation in 1991, claiming to be the "real world's champion." Shortly after the turn of the new year, in the January 1992 *Royal Rumble*, Flair made good on his boast. He became the WWF Champion.

Flair's road to the title was typical of his scheming ways. The way he won it, however, typifies what a superb athlete he is.

Hulk Hogan had the championship title, but interference by Flair caused its loss to the Undertaker. A few days later, Hogan reclaimed the belt, but again Flair interfered, and a seemingly incorrect ruling by WWF President Jack Tunney resulted in the title being vacated. Tunney decreed that the winner of the *Royal Rumble*'s 30-man over-the-top battle royal would be declared champion.

In this battle royal, wrestlers draw numbers to determine the sequence in which they will go into the ring. Nos. 1 and 2 enter the ring first. Every two minutes thereafter, the wrestler with the next number in sequence enters. The winner of the battle is the last man to remain in the ring. As things usually turn out, the early men to enter seldom last to the later stages of the battle because they are tired when new entrants are fresh. Never in the history of the *Royal Rumble* battle royal, in fact, had any of the first five men to enter lasted to the final moments. Flair changed all that.

The Million Dollar Man and the British Bulldog were the first two wrestlers to step between the ropes.

He's Slick Ric, the man who loves to party. Ric Flair won the 1992 *Royal Rumble*.

With shocking speed, the Bulldog eliminated DiBiase. And in came Flair. He and the Bulldog fought fiercely and brilliantly. The other warriors began arriving. Still Flair and the Bulldog remained, although men began to be thrown over the top rope with abandon. The Bulldog, in fact, lasted 22 minutes before Flair ousted him. All the while, Flair continued his quest. He hacked, chopped and slammed away at other combatants, who in turn pummeled him viciously. It was Flair against Haku, Flair against the Big Boss Man, Flair against Rowdy Roddy Piper, Flair against Jake "The Snake" Roberts, Flair against everybody.

"I love it, I love it, I love it." Ric Flair after winning the title.

WWF television commentators Gorilla Monsoon and Bobby "The Brain" Heenan repeatedly marveled at Flair's staying power. Heenan, in particular, was overjoyed, because he was Flair's booster.

Shouting into the announcer's microphone, even though Flair could not hear him, Heenan urged his favorite to stay away from the fighting and rest whenever he could. Flair didn't need Heenan's advice. A crafty veteran, Flair took every chance to rest, avoiding combat when he tired, although always looking for an opportunity to strike at someone when the chance presented itself. It seemed that whenever an area of the ring was open and free of combatants, Flair could be found there, seeking a few precious seconds of rest. He managed these respites adeptly. It was the key to his survival.

Weight:
242 pounds

From:
Charlotte, North Carolina

Birthday:
January 6

Favorite finishing hold:
Figure-four leglock, but also many others

Trademark:
Technical expert but perhaps most unscrupulous man in the ring

Favorite quote:
"I'm a Lear-jet-flying, caviar-eating son of a gun."

Goal:
Everything his heart desires

> **The best-looking women, the finest champagnes, the most luxurious cars — that's my style. That's Ric Flair.**

Even the great Hulk Hogan feels the agonizing pain of Ric Flair's figure-four leglock. Flair's version of this hold is the most effective in the WWF.

Even so, as the ring filled with sweaty, muscular bodies, Flair could not help being caught up in the fray and — even his many detractors admit — acquitted himself marvelously. Dripping with perspiration, his chest heaving with exhaustion, Flair took all his foes could throw at him and gave back more, always, as is his style, opting for a cheap shot if he could get away with it. As the battle raged, Flair repeatedly demonstrated his ability to use what may be a wider variety of weapons than possessed by any other wrestler. As bodies flew around him and men slugged it out for all their worth, Flair ended up on the mat, where Greg "The Hammer"

Valentine applied the figure-four leglock on him. Flair writhed in agony as Valentine put on the pressure. Observers marveled that Flair could resist the hold while a couple of dozen wrestlers stood over him, tearing at one another like tigers. Most wrestlers would have been doomed in such a situation. How Flair wasn't trampled is almost beyond belief.

Again and again, the finest athletes in the WWF tried to shove, throw or wrestle Flair over the top rope. Hooking his legs into the ropes, grabbing the strands, clawing and wiggling, Flair tenaciously resisted. Try as they might, not even foes such as the Undertaker, Sgt. Slaughter and Jake Roberts could get Flair out of the ring. At times it looked as if he would collapse from exhaustion, but each time he managed to rally.

In the end, it was Flair, Sid Justice and Hulk Hogan left in the ring. As Flair contested Hogan, Justice struck from behind and eliminated the Hulkster. It appeared as if Flair and the huge Justice — who entered

the ring next to last and was thus fresh — would vie for the honors. But as Flair pushed on Justice, the Hulkster reached up and yanked him to the floor. Inadvertently, Hogan had created a new champion.

Flair had beaten all the odds. He had accomplished what no other man had ever done — starting the *Royal Rumble* battle royal almost from scratch and emerging the winner. That alone would be enough to put him in the WWF history books. But Flair took it another step higher. He ended up not only winning the battle royal but also winning the WWF Championship Belt.

"Woooooh, baby," crowed Flair afterward, as he celebrated his victory with his adviser Mr. Perfect and toady Bobby Heenan. "I said it. I'm the true champion. Some people didn't believe Ric Flair. Now they've got no choice. And I don't have to say anything. Because this belt I'm wearing, this gold around my waist, says it all. Ric Flair, WWF Champion. And that's the real deal." ∎

Flair roughs up Haku at the 1992 *Royal Rumble*. No one else has ever entered the ring as early as Flair and lasted to the end.

Sid Justice

Weight:
318 pounds

From:
West Memphis, Arkansas

Birthday:
July 4

Favorite finishing hold:
The powerbomb

Trademark:
Brutality in the ring

Favorite quote:
"Justice will be served."

Goal:
Justice for all

....

Sid Justice puts pressure on Jake "The Snake" Roberts with a powerful headlock.

id Justice had everybody fooled when he came to the WWF. He talked a lot about being a farmboy from Arkansas, with old-fashioned values. From his later actions, it was only talk. Only that.

"I was raised on a farm in the country," he said. "My grandfather taught me that the land was sacred. He showed me that the people who work the land to raise food for others are the salt of the earth. I'm bigger and stronger than most of those people. I've seen lots more of the world than most of them, too. But I never let myself forget that they are the strongest people in the world. Their lives are tough. I know about it — getting up in the dark to milk the cows, going out in the hot sun to cut the hay before it rains and throwing hay bales around even when your arms ache."

Sid can keep his opponents at bay, letting them tire themselves as they strive vainly to reach him.

Speaking of throwing things around, Sid Justice does it pretty well on his opponents. He is huge, yet lean and mean. His musculature is distributed so evenly on his body that he looks lithe despite his impressive weight. He is sinewy, which adds to the thrusting power that enables him to toss opponents with devastating force. Given his height and the length of his limbs, adversaries have a difficult time getting at him.

Sid Justice radiates physical and spiritual power. Never was this more evident than when Jake "The Snake"

Roberts and the Undertaker destroyed the happiness of Macho Man Randy Savage and Elizabeth at their *Summer-Slam* wedding reception. Elizabeth was being terrorized by Jake and his cobra. Macho Man Randy Savage was down, beaten in an Undertaker Pearl Harbor attack. Justice appeared, and the villains fled.

Justice's true colors, however, eventually surfaced. He became greedy for early fame. He lusted for the WWF Title. In the 1992 *Royal Rumble*, at which the final survivor was to be given the title, Justice turned on his friend and ally Hulk Hogan and ousted him from the ring. Still, Justice didn't get the title because he, in turn, was ousted by Flair, with help from Hogan. From the arena floor Hulk grabbed Sid's arm and yanked him as Slick Ric shoved him. Justice's anger was turned not at Flair, but at Hogan. He became one of the Hulkster's most bitter enemies. ■

Justice had everyone fooled into thinking he was an honest farmboy. Instead, he is greedy and unscrupulous.

A former WWF Tag Team Champion, the British Bulldog is an all-around phenomenon. He is an adept aerial artist, given to striking from the air with bone-jarring flying dropkicks and flying clotheslines. He has mountains of muscle on his compact frame, giving him the power equal to those competitors in the WWF who tower over him. One such competitor is the Warlord, whom the British Bulldog went up against in *WrestleMania VII* in Los Angeles, California. The Warlord, a monster of a man, perhaps one of the most powerful men alive, was out to bend the Bulldog into submission with the full nelson. The Bulldog used his own strength to counter the Warlord, then finished him off with the running powerslam that is his patented finisher.

"I'll remember that match for the rest of my life," says the Bulldog. "Not only was it a *WrestleMania* event, but I was up against a man who probably is the most intimidating opponent I've ever faced. There were times I felt as if I needed to stand on a stepladder to get a shot at his ugly mug. It was a real test for me. Usually, I know that I can outmuscle my opponents as well as beat them technically and with agility. But outmuscle the Warlord? I knew that couldn't happen. What I wanted to find out was whether or not I could match him muscle for muscle, even if not pound for pound. Well, I did. I think he was surprised. He's so used to pushing people around. Well, when it came to push, I shoved

harder. When I hit him with the running powerslam, I immediately knew it was all over."

Nobody in the WWF executes the running powerslam like the Bulldog. With his speed and power, this move becomes lethal. And it's a beauty to watch. The Bulldog dashes at his foe, scooping him up in massive arms,

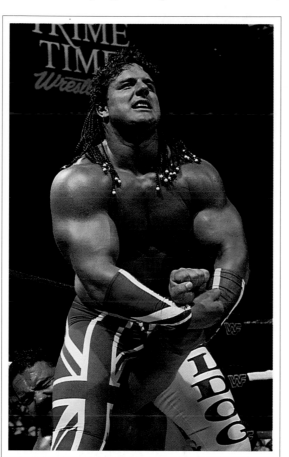

Above: Using his prodigious strength, the Bulldog puts all his oomph into an armbar.

....

Opposite: The British Bulldog proudly wears his country's colors into the WWF ring.

gripping him tight and then smashing him to the canvas. All of the Bulldog's weight lands atop the victim, squashing the wind out of him, knocking him half-conscious and ending the match.

Weight:
275 pounds

From:
Leeds, England

Birthday:
December 12

Favorite finishing hold:
Running powerslam

Trademark:
A massive yet chiseled physique

Favorite quote:
"Rule Britannia"

Goal:
To bring a WWF title home to England

The British Bulldog

Once he has an adversary down on the mat, the Bulldog goes to work on him. The Bulldog's tactics maximize his muscular might.

On December 3, 1991, the Bulldog and Warlord met again. This time the Bulldog used speed as well as power to defeat his huge adversary, pinning him after a flying crucifix.

The Bulldog is strong genetically, but he didn't get his impressive muscles by taking it easy. Around wrestling circles, he is known as a man who puts in endless hours at the gym. He pumps iron with a passion. "I'd probably do it even if I wasn't wrestling," he says.

"When I first started wrestling," he explains, "I knew I'd meet opponents who were much larger than I was. I'm not what you'd call short, but there are men in the WWF who look as tall as oaks. I realized I had to bulk up to the maximum to be able to handle opponents like that. So, in addition to working on my

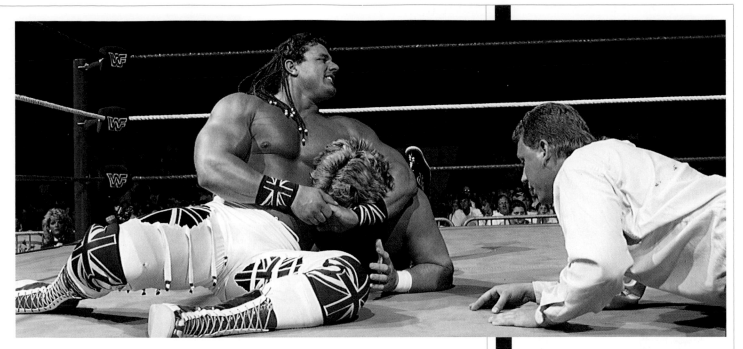

wrestling moves and maneuvers, I learned all I could about building my body. And I put it to practice."

It's not surprising, therefore, that the British Bulldog is a fan of the WWF's sister organization, the World Bodybuilding Federation. "Those guys — the ones who compete in the WBF — make me want to work harder in the gym. They're impressive."

Hailing from England, the Bulldog wears Britain's national colors into the ring. "I'm proud of my national heritage," he says. "That's why I'm sky-high about the way the WWF has taken off in the UK. When I go there on tour, not only do I get a chance to go home, but I get to wrestle live in front of my fellow countrymen. The only way they used to see me was on television. Now I'm able to do my best for them in person. Wrestling in the UK has been one of the proudest moments in my life. It's a dream come true for the British Bulldog."

Of course, the Bulldog doesn't forget his faithful fans in the United States and Canada as well as elsewhere in the world. "I'll never forget my fans in North America," he says.

"They've been with me through thick and thin. I know they've never let me down, and I'll never let them down. They're the greatest."

"Even so," says the Bulldog, "it would be nice to bring an individual WWF title back to England. My big dream is to win the title in front of a British audience. Maybe that will never happen, but you never know. Meanwhile, I'll take any shot I can get at a championship belt, whatever side of the Atlantic it's on. I wore the tag team belt once, but that meant I was a co-holder. My ambition is to have a belt that's all mine. That way I'll know I've reached the peak of my ability."

The Bulldog has fans everywhere pulling for him. With his ready smile and affable manner, he appeals to fans of all ages. They are also drawn to him because he is confident yet unassuming. Bravado and bluster are not the Bulldog's way. He is a sportsman in the ring, not given to cheap shots. But if someone tries to nail him with a dirty tactic, he is more than willing to let his fists do the talking for him. He is, after all, a dog with not just a bark but also a bite. ■

Working on the mat, the Bulldog tenaciously wears down his opponent with a variety of holds to render him vulnerable to a pinfall.

. . . .

❝ I don't think I've ever felt a more severe impact than when the Bulldog hit me with a running powerslam ❞ says one former opponent, who asks to remain anonymous.

Weight:
249 pounds

From:
Stone Mountain, Georgia

Birthday:
May 30

Favorite finishing hold:
The DDT

Trademark:
Deceit

Favorite quote:
"Never trust a snake."

Goal:
To be worse than the devil

Never trust a snake. That's what people everywhere say about Jake "The Snake" Roberts. And that's what Jake says about himself. Typical of this bizarre, intrinsically evil individual, he is proud of it.

"Oh yes, my man," says Roberts, "never trust a snake. That goes for snakes that wriggle around on their bellies. And that goes even more for the greatest snake of all — me, Jake the Snake."

This type of outlook on life says it all about Jake Roberts. He is a man unto himself, a man seemingly without scruples who delights in committing the most atrocious acts he can devise. He thrives on indulging in shocking behavior. And he seems to live to hurt others, to destroy happiness and blight the lives of whomever — for reasons known only to his serpentine mind — he targets for destruction.

Deep within Jake there seems to be an abiding hatred for all around him, a darkness as black as that in a shadowy temple out of fantasy. Only in Jake's case it isn't fantasy. He is the most venomous individual imaginable. It would not be at all surprising

Jake's companions are a deadly king cobra (*inset*) and a huge python. These serpents may be dangerous, but not nearly as treacherous as the man who holds them.

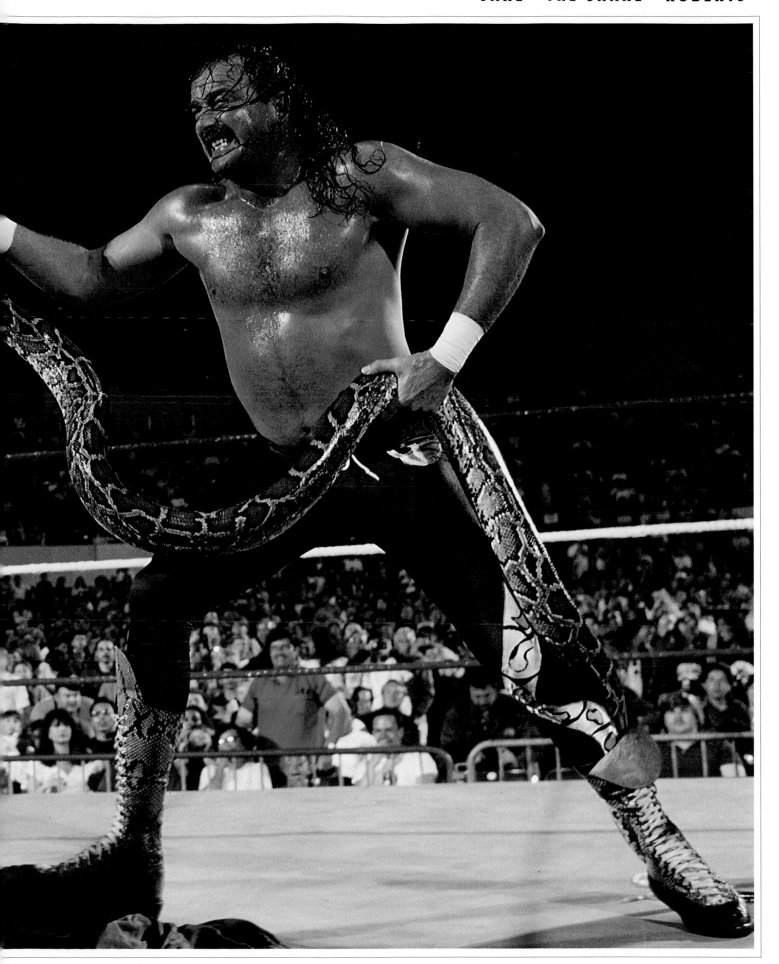

One of the most shocking events in WWF history was when Jake the Snake unleashed his king cobra and had it bite Randy Savage.

if we found out that the blood coursing through his veins was poisonous.

Roberts admires the traits he believes snakes possess. He likes the idea that in Western society snakes are considered a symbol of evil, although in other parts of the world they are not thought of so badly. He revels in the fact that some snakes — by no means the majority — are venomous. Jake also prides in himself on being cold-blooded, like a snake — and that he, like all snakes, is a natural predator.

"STEP UP, MY MAN"

"People wonder about me," says Jake. "What makes me the way I am? Well, they think they know me, even if they don't know what makes me tick. They don't know me. If they could look into

my mind, their souls would shrivel. They would have nightmares for the rest of their lives. Oh no, people, you haven't begun to learn about Jake 'The Snake' Roberts. I am capable of things that you never could imagine or want to imagine. Step up, my man. Step up and shake hands with Jake 'The Snake' Roberts. Come on, shake hands with the devil."

If anybody doubts Jake's words, consider what he did to Macho Man Randy Savage and his lovely bride, Elizabeth, the First Lady of the WWF. Hark back to *SummerSlam* last year. At that event, the Macho Man and Elizabeth were married in a splendid ceremony in center ring. Afterward the happy couple celebrated at a gala wedding reception, to which they had invited many of their WWF friends.

They did not invite Jake. Why

should they have? They did not invite the feared Undertaker, with whom Jake had formed a dark alliance. But the two of them, foul to the core, showed up. Jake, indeed, had a present for the bride — a present that was pure poison. It was a deadly cobra.

With a cruel smile on his face, his eyes glittering with warped glee, Jake menaced Elizabeth with the serpent while the Undertaker jumped Savage and pounded him into oblivion. Repeatedly, Jake threatened the helpless beauty with his object of death. Elizabeth screamed, quivering with shock and disbelief. She was in the grasp of pure unadulterated terror.

The Snake's act cast a pall upon the marriage of Savage and Elizabeth, a match supposedly made in heaven. But Jake still was not finished. Luring Savage from the WWF announcer's booth into the ring by taunting him during a televised event, Jake attacked him from behind, beat him and then produced a huge king cobra. At Jake's command, the reptile sank its fangs deep into Savage's arm. Randy writhed in pain. Then, after fitfully trying to get his hands on Jake, Randy collapsed. Jake later said he thought the cobra was devenomized. It apparently was not. Only quick medical treatment saved Savage from disaster. So shocked by Jake's action was WWF President Jack Tunney that he banned him from ever again bringing a reptile to ringside.

Randy wanted revenge but had to wait. He had been suspended from the ring by Tunney after losing a retirement match to the Ultimate Warrior. Finally at the *Survivor Series*, Tunney reinstated Savage. On December 3, he and Jake met. Thirsting for vengeance, Savage was a whirlwind. He stopped Jake with a flying elbow off the top rope and scored a pin. But Savage wanted more than victory. He wanted to beat the devil out of Jake. That was a mistake. In the end, it was Jake who did the beating, repeatedly hitting Savage with DDTs, then manhandling Elizabeth when she ran into the ring to try to protect her man.

Jake did not always seem like such a demon. It may be, however, that the darkness always lurked within him, waiting for a time to reveal itself. His taunting eyes and cynical smile betrayed a mockery of the rest of the world. Jake brooded and pondered the darkness that gripped him. Secretly, he began to revel in it. Sooner or later, the evil in Jake had to surface. And so it did. Jake "The Snake" Roberts has become a man who is the devil himself. ∎

Jake's fascination with serpents goes back as long as he can remember. "I used to play with snakes when I was a little boy back in Georgia," he says. "I found in them things to admire, yes indeed."

Trying to rend Savage limb from limb, Jake yanks on his hair and tries to pound his head into the ring.

Sgt. Slaughter

Weight:
310 pounds

From:
South Carolina

Birthday:
May 25

Favorite finishing hold:
Camel clutch

Trademark:
A rugged military style

Favorite quote:
"My country, right or wrong."

Goal:
To be the best American he can be

Standing before the Iwo Jima Memorial in Washington, D.C., Sgt. Slaughter salutes the proud history of the U.S. Marine Corps.

Sgt. Slaughter is a prime example of the fact that anyone — even the best of us — can go wrong at any time. He is also an example of how the worst transgressors can be redeemed if they want it badly enough.

Slaughter wanted the WWF Championship Title more than anything he could imagine. A patriot, he sold out his country and sided with General Adnan and Colonel Mustafa, whose ruthless ways Sarge believed could get him the prize. It worked. He beat the Ultimate Warrior and took the gold. But at *WrestleMania VII*, he lost the belt to Hulk Hogan, who had decided to go after Slaughter to defend the honor of the United States.

Again Hogan, with the Warrior, challenged Slaughter. They went against the Sarge and his two allies at *SummerSlam*. Slaughter and his cohorts were pounded as bad as Baghdad. Defeated, Slaughter's allies turned on him. It was the best thing that could have happened to this patriot who, blinded by ambition, had become a turncoat.

Distraught, realizing what he had done to himself and his country, Slaughter went into seclusion. He was racked by self-doubt, despondent and ready to toss in the towel.

915-1934 × SANTO·DOMINGO·1916-1924 × WORLD·WAR·I·1917-1918·BELL

IN·HONOR·AND·MEMORY
OF·THE·MEN·OF·THE
UNITED·STATES·MARINE·CORPS
WHO·HAVE·GIVEN
THEIR·LIVES·TO·THEIR·COUNTRY
SINCE·10·NOVEMBER·1775

However, he touched on his inner strength. He realized there was a chance, if only minimal, to redeem himself. Brimming with emotion, he roared, "I want my country back."

He got it. Slowly and painfully, he began his road back to his country. He visited the sites that memorialize the spirit of the USA — the Iwo Jima Memorial, honoring the nation's finest fighting force, the U.S. Marines; Arlington National Cemetery; and the White House. He went back to the people, leading school children in the Pledge of Allegiance to Old Glory.

"Fly the flag high, fly it proud and defend it with your life."

Then came a night when Slaughter was put to the test. Hacksaw Jim Duggan, another patriot, was ambushed by the Nasty Boys. He was at their mercy. Slaughter rushed to Duggan's rescue. For Slaughter it was the end of a tragic period and the beginning of a new life. He had his country back. He had a partner who would help him keep Old Glory flying proudly.

Their first targets were the Nasty Boys. Said Slaughter, "Nasty Boys, you've got a war on your hands because you're a threat to the USA. You like to jump people and brutalize people; you think might makes right. This war is on the streets, right here on the home front. Hacksaw and I are gonna make those streets safe. We're gonna wipe you into the gutter." Slaughter and Hacksaw did just that. ■

Slaughter's bodyslam is a real stunner.

The Beverly Brothers

Combined weight:
558 pounds

From:
Shaker Heights, Ohio

Birthdays:
Beau, March 22;
Blake, June 11

Favorite finishing hold:
The Beverly Bomb

Trademark:
King-sized spoiled brats

Favorite quote:
"The world is our oyster."

Goal:
To wear the tag team gold

The Beverly Brothers, who were raised among the mansions of the posh Cleveland suburb of Shaker Heights, grew up spoiled. "We always got everything we wanted," says Beau. "First it was candy and toys."

"Then it was cars and girls," smirks Blake. "I had two 'vettes. Beau had a Jag and a T-Bird. And we were only 16 years old."

The Beverly Brothers, Beau and Blake, love to double-team opponents and are good at getting away with it.

That's not malarkey. The Beverly Brothers indeed had everything. By the time they were 12 years of age, they had seen more of the world and stayed in more luxury hotels than most people even read about in a life-

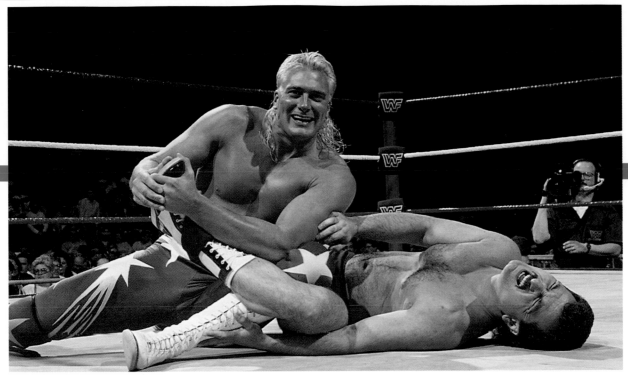

time. Their parents coddled them in every way possible.

Now, for the first time, the Beverly Brothers want something more than they ever have — and so far they haven't been able to get it. It's not theirs for the asking, because it is the WWF Tag Team Championship. Being so spoiled, the Beverly Brothers are enraged that the tag team belts are not theirs. Instead of throwing a typical tantrum, they are taking out their frustrations on their opponents.

This fact is not lost on the Genius, the Beverly Brothers' scholarly manager. He feeds their frustration, knowing it will make them meaner and meaner. Always underhanded, the Beverly Brothers have become even more sneaky under the tutelage of the Genius.

The Beverly Brothers have smothered most of their competition. This helps them relieve their anger but also has taken them toward the prize they seek. The better their record, the more victories they notch up, the better chance they feel they will have at a tag team title shot.

The vicious streak in the Beverly Brothers is evident in their finishing hold. When they get an opponent on the ropes, they double-team him. The poor unfortunate is hurled into the air, horizontal to the mat and face-down. Propelled by a handful of his hair, the victim is smashed face-first into the canvas.

Beau and Blake Beverly feel they are on the verge of their goal. "We've gone up against those goofball Bushwhackers," says Beau, "and we gave them a lesson in tag team wrestling. We looked great."

"Now, we feel that they should just give us a shot at the tag team title," says Blake. "After all, we deserve it. It's our due." The championship belts, however, have to be earned. ■

Beau Beverly smirks gleefully as he makes an opponent grimace and writhe in pain.

....

Beau and Blake

Weight:
260 pounds

From:
Seasonal residences

Birthday:
January 18

Favorite finishing hold:
The Million Dollar Dream sleeperhold

Trademark:
Large amounts of cash carried to the ring

Favorite quote:
"Everybody's got a price for the Million Dollar Man."

Goal:
To get even richer at everyone's expense

At first glance, you would think the Million Dollar Man Ted DiBiase has everything. His income seems endless, although no one knows its source. Some fans believe his father made it big in oil. Be that as it may, he has all that money can buy. Seasonally, he moves between palatial homes in Palm Beach, Aruba, Kennebunkport, Aspen and a host of other places. Some people say he has lost count of his mansions. Ted DiBiase eats at the best restaurants, even though each home has a staff of chefs trained in Paris. He has a fleet of luxury cars, all custom-built. Fly first class? No way. He has a Jetstream and a Lear. He never lifts a hand to do anything. He has servants aplenty.

In the squared circle, DiBiase, a truly seasoned veteran, also has all the assets. He is deceptively strong. Even his many critics admit he is one of the most adept wrestlers ever. There is not a hold or a move he doesn't know.

On any given night, the Million Dollar Man Ted DiBiase, a superb wrestler who is deceptively strong, can beat any opponent.

You would think that, with all these advantages, DiBiase would be satisfied. He isn't. For some reason he feels he has to flaunt his success to cow and crush everyone else. He has no need to turn mean in the ring. His wrestling ability could pull him through, but he likes to beat on people.

He likes to crush people psychologically, too. DiBiase feels the need to use his money in order to make peo-

Above: Once the Million Dollar Man clamps on his Million Dollar Dream, it's lights out. *Opposite:* DiBiase scores with a vicious powerslam. *Inset:* DiBiase delights in stuffing a $100 bill into the mouth of a defeated opponent.

ple crawl. For some reason, he enjoys preying on the common person's financial needs, making them humble themselves for cash.

No one suffered more at the hands of DiBiase than Virgil, his former bodyguard and valet. Trying to support his indigent family back home, Virgil literally cleaned the dung from DiBiase's shoes. But, with the counseling of Rowdy Roddy Piper, Virgil regained his dignity. He even beat DiBiase and took the Million Dollar Belt, which was crafted by the world's most expensive jewelers. Virgil eventually lost the belt back to DiBiase, but only because DiBiase had paid off the Repo Man to interfere in their match.

A high point in DiBiase's career occurred early in 1992 when he and IRS, now known as Money Inc., claimed the WWF Tag Team Championship. Being a champion changed him not a bit. He remains greedy for more success. ∎

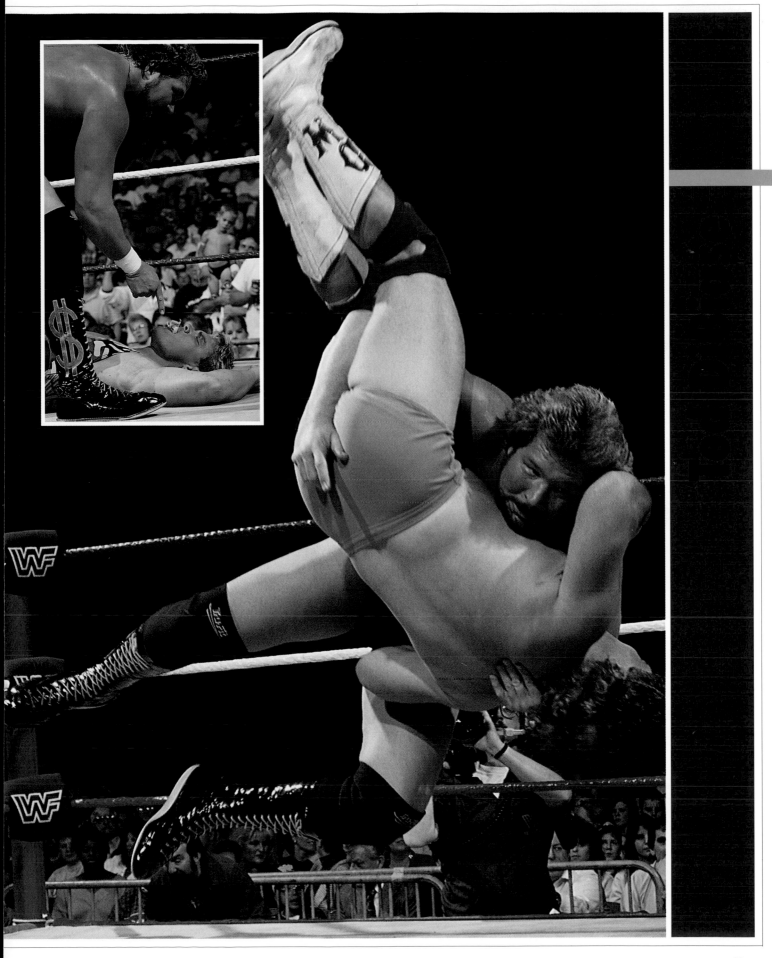

Bret "Hit Man" Hart

Weight:
234 pounds

From:
Calgary, Alberta, Canada

Birthday:
July 2

Favorite finishing hold:
Sharpshooter

Trademark:
Excellence of execution

Favorite quote:
"You're in my sights."

Goal:
To perfect all aspects of his wrestling technique

The battle between Bret Hart and Mr. Perfect at *SummerSlam 1991* was a spectacular wrestling display.

Bret "Hit Man" Hart, who hails from a famed wrestling family, has held the WWF Intercontinental Title and has been a co-holder of the WWF Tag Team Title with former partner and brother-in-law Jim Neidhart.

Bret is known for his great mastery of scientific wrestling techniques, largely the result of early schooling by his father, Stu, an elder statesman of wrestling. Perhaps the greatest exhibition of Bret's scientific talents came at *SummerSlam 1991* when he beat

another technical expert, Mr. Perfect, for the Intercontinental Title.

Both wrestlers were in peak physical condition and ready to go all out. Perfect, however, was aided by the presence of his manager at the time, Coach, who was always ready to

interfere or distract the referee.

Bret took the lead early, confusing Perfect by running the ropes and bounding off them, then going to the air and catching him in a stunning crucifix. Perfect was then hit with a cross-bodyblock and spun over by a sunset flip. He then seemed to decide he would lose the match — but by WWF rules, not the title — by returning to the dressing room and taking a count-out. Bret would have none of it. He chased Perfect, smacked him with a solid punch and threw him back into the ring.

The match changed momentum as the two battlers took their fight outside the ring. Mr. Perfect, at his best in such situations, chopped Bret down and then, as humiliation, used him as a human stepladder to climb back into the ring. Wrong move, Mr. P! The act infuriated Bret. He rejoined the battle and dazzled Perfect, countering his finest moves and kicking out when Mr. P tried for a pin.

Bret then tried his Sharpshooter, a unique version of the leg grapevine, in hopes of gaining a submission. Fearing defeat, Perfect's manager jumped to the ring apron and tried to distract the referee. Making one of his few mistakes during the match, Bret left Perfect and popped his manager. Seizing the chance, Mr. P mounted an assault on Bret, dropping legs to his chest. In a display of exceptionally quick thinking and skill, Bret blocked a leg, held onto Mr. Perfect's foot and executed the Sharpshooter. The belt belonged to Bret Hart. ■

The victory was made even more memorable for Bret because his parents were at ringside.

Bret "Hit Man" Hart personifies "cool." He's cool-headed in the ring, too. The Hit Man truly is a thinking man's wrestler.

....

The Mountie

Weight:
245 pounds

From:
Canada

Birthday:
June 13

Favorite finishing hold:
The carotid control technique

Trademark:
Using an electric cattle prod on opponents

Favorite quote:
"I always get my man."

Goal:
To shock the WWF

Managed by Jimmy "Mouth of the South" Hart, the Mountie managed to cop the Intercontinental Title from Bret "Hit Man" Hart in January 1992 when, against physician's orders, Bret went to the ring with a 104°F fever. The Mountie did not hold the Intercontinental Title long, much to the delight of many WWF fans, who accuse him of enforcing the law for his own ends and using police brutality.

Basically, the Mountie is a bully who hides behind his uniform. His favorite tactic is to shock opponents with his cattle prod. It is a vicious act, typical of the Mountie.

As smug as he is mean, the Mountie claims once he is on an opponent's trail, he is doomed. "The Mountie always gets his man," says he. "No one can possibly escape me. Those who try will receive even more punishment at the hands of the Mountie."

Since he donned his scarlet uniform, the Mountie has shown that he is totally without scruples and an absolute hypocrite. He claims to enforce the laws internationally but breaks the laws of sportsmanship in the squared circle any chance he gets. He asserts he is out to take down lawbreakers but associates with the worst rulebreakers in the WWF, and his manager often acts like a thief. The Mountie says no one is above the law, but he acts as if it does not apply to him.

The cruelty of the Mountie is demonstrated by the fact that he uses holds normally applied to control combative suspects in order to hurt other wrestlers. His carotid control technique, which strikes at a key artery in the neck, can cause extreme pain, which the Mountie seems to enjoy delivering.

While the Mountie likes to dish out punishment, he doesn't like to receive

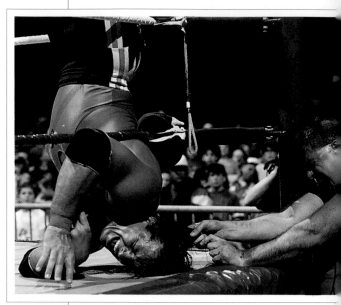

Above: The Mountie uses typical dirty tactics against Bret "Hit Man" Hart. *Opposite:* Tito Santana, before he became El Matador, is jolted by the Mountie's cattle prod.

it. Typically, if he gets in trouble between the ropes, he will look for Jimmy Hart to interfere or distract the referee by jumping about and yapping through his megaphone.

One must admit, however, that the Mountie does seem to have a knack for some of wrestling's more difficult holds and maneuvers. He is quite aerial and can deliver a flying dropkick with blinding speed. His mat work, even without control techniques, is admirable, even if his behavior is not. Thus, the Mountie poses a distinct threat to all his opponents, even if, despite his bragging, he does not always get his man. ∎

66 I am the Mountie. **99**

Anyone who crosses the Big Boss Man is likely to end up a victim of the Boss Man slam, a thunderous version of the powerslam, and then find himself handcuffed to the ring ropes.

Here it comes — the Boss Man Slam. With the Boss Man's 337 pounds coming down on opponents, few of them recover from this thunderous power move.

You can expect no nonsense from the Big Boss Man. He's young, but he's been through the school of hard knocks. You don't run herd on a bunch of Georgia convicts in the Big House or on a chain gang without getting tough. The Big Boss Man brings his unique brand of law enforcement to the WWF. He patrols the ring, seeking out all those who break the rules and taking them to task.

For the Big Boss Man, 1991 was an especially eventful year in the WWF. At *WrestleMania VII*, he had a chance to take the Intercontinental Title away from then-champion Mr. Perfect. However, Perfect's allies, the Barbarian and Haku, interfered and caused the Boss Man to win the match by disqualification. A champion cannot lose his belt by disqualification, so Perfect retained the title.

Next, the Big Boss Man crossed horns with a man who also professes to uphold the law but really abuses it. He is the Mountie, who with the Nasty Boys blindsided the Boss Man during one of his matches. After they all pounded the Georgia lawman, the Mountie picked up his infamous cattle prod and jolted him with 4,000 volts of electricity. However, the Big Boss Man had his revenge at *SummerSlam*. He encountered the Mountie in a match with a special stipulation. The loser had to go to jail. As things turned out, the Mountie spent the night in the cooler.

After that, the Boss Man tangled with IRS, also known as Irwin R. Schyster. Like the Mountie, IRS pretends to uphold the law, in his case, tax law. The Boss Man says he is tired of people like IRS and the Mountie using the law to abuse people.

"The only way to enforce the law is

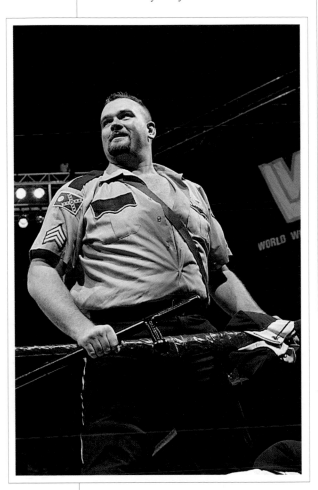

He's the Big Boss Man and no one to fool with. He sternly and objectively enforces the law in the WWF's squared circle.

the right way," he says. "You've got to be tough, sure, but you've got to be fair. And that's the way the Big Boss Man is. I don't bother anybody who walks a straight path. But if you take the crooked one, the Boss Man's gonna see that you serve hard time." ■

Weight:
337 pounds

From:
Cobb County, Georgia

Birthday:
May 2

Favorite finishing hold:
The Boss Man slam

Trademark:
Love for the law

Favorite quote:
"Do the crime, serve hard time."

Goal:
To preserve the law in the WWF

Andre the Giant

Weight:
520 pounds

From:
Grenoble, France

Birthday:
May 14

Trademark:
Sheer size

Favorite finishing hold:
Anything he wants to use

Favorite quote:
"I am the true giant of the WWF."

Goal:
To be remembered as the "Eighth Wonder of the World"

There is no one quite like Andre the Giant in the WWF — probably not in the entire world. Andre is indeed "The Eighth Wonder of the World." He is as mountainous as the French Alps from which he hails. Over the years, Andre has become a legend in the WWF, feared by some but loved and respected by many others.

"Andre the Giant is one of a kind," says Hulk Hogan. "His courage is as big as his heart. To my way of thinking, man, Andre stands for something really special."

Not everyone agrees. "Andre is useless. That's all I've got to say," snaps Bobby "The Brain" Heenan.

No wonder he says that. Heenan for a time was Andre's manager and tried to lead him astray. But Andre eventually learned that Heenan was merely using him and cut their ties. After a hiatus from the WWF, Andre returned at *WrestleMania VII*. Heenan was one of the several unscrupulous managers Andre rejected after they all scrambled to get his contract. Angering Heenan even more was the fact that at *WrestleMania VII* Andre came to the aid of the Big Boss Man, who was beset by Mr. Perfect, the Barbarian and Haku, all members of the Heenan family.

Another manager rejected by Andre was Jimmy "Mouth of the South" Hart. Angered, he set the Giant up for an attack by the monstrous Earthquake, who focused his brutal attention on Andre's knee, which had been giving him problems. Andre had to

undergo reconstructive surgery. Whether he will wrestle again is open to question, but even if he doesn't, his mighty presence will always be felt in the squared circle.

Andre is a quiet man, not given to much talking. When he talks, however, people listen. "I've spent many years in the WWF," he says in a low,

Andre the Giant has had his share of injuries during his long, illustrious career. He has fought pain as valiantly as he has battled enemies within the squared circle.

rumbling voice. "They have been the best years of my life. Even if I never wrestle again, the World Wrestling Federation will remain in my heart."

That is very well said, Eighth Wonder of the World! ■

> " I've always looked up to Andre the Giant. Years ago, when I first came to the WWF, I really didn't know what was going on. To tell the truth, I was nervous. Andre took me aside and set me straight. He's a true friend. "
> EL MATADOR

When he came to the WWF in April 1991, IRS immediately focused his attention on Superfly Jimmy Snuka, who doesn't have a cheating bone in his body. Nevertheless, IRS took him to the squared circle and audited him but good.

. . . .

IRS is out to get you, says he. This wily man with the briefcase thinks almost everyone is a tax cheat.

In tough economic times, nobody likes the tax man. That goes double for IRS, Irwin R. Schyster. He delights in putting the squeeze on people, making them squirm and wringing out their last coin. In his eyes, everyone but the people he likes — unsavory sorts such as the Million Dollar Man Ted DiBiase — is a tax cheat. And he treats them accordingly.

"I don't care where you live, in New York, Montreal or London," says IRS. "You're all a bunch of no-good, money-grubbing tax cheats. You think you can take off your flea-infested dog or your new television as deductions. Think again. I'll go over every letter and number in your tax returns. And I'll find those phony deductions. The same goes for not recording your income. Think you can get away from IRS by taking cash? That's the laugh of the year. I'm going to drag you into my office, make you show receipts and then go over everything you bought. Then I'll ask you where the money came from. And you won't be able to tell me."

An audit by IRS, who is a polished as well as an unscrupulous wrestler, is not pleasant to see. He stalks his opponent, sneaking in cheap shots whenever possible. Once he thinks a man is weakening, IRS puts him in agonizing abdominal stretches. "If you try to stretch your dollar, I'm going to stretch you," he says. After that, IRS's victim is likely to be targeted with the Write-off, a devastating fall-away slam.

IRS achieved the greatest success of his stingy life when, early in 1992, he and the Million Dollar Man Ted DiBiase, known as Money Inc., captured the WWF Tag Team Title. That conquest made IRS very happy, indeed, because it enhanced his powers in the WWF. And he enjoyed fully working with Ted DiBiase. "No tax cuts for the wealthy," said IRS of his favorite partner. "It's the little people who have to pay and if I have anything to say about it, they'll pay through the nose." ■

Weight:
248 pounds

From:
Washington, D.C.

Birthday:
April 15

Favorite finishing hold:
The Write-off

Trademark:
The briefcase he carries

Favorite quote:
"Pay me now, or pay me later."

Goal:
To audit everybody in the world

IRS tried to settle the Big Boss Man's accounts in the ring, but the Boss Man eventually sent him packing.

IRS (Irwin R. Schyster)

Combined Weight:
572 pounds

From:
Chicago, Illinois

Birthdays:
Unknown

Favorite finishing hold:
The Doomsday Device

Trademark:
Ability to go toe-to-toe with anyone

Favorite quote:
"What a rushhh."

Goal:
To get even tougher

Right: Hawk and Animal. *Opposite:* Legion of Doom executes the Doomsday Device.

Hawk and Animal of the Legion of Doom, who have held the WWF Tag Team Title, are scary to look at. They are even scarier to see in action. Take their finishing tactic, for example. From the top turnbuckle, Hawk flies through the air and clotheslines the opponent off Animal's shoulders. The poor target lands with near-paralyzing impact, an easy mark for a pin.

"Nobody gets up when we hit 'em with our Doomsday Device," says Hawk. "That's right," adds Animal. "When I get 'em up on my shoulders and you come sailing through the air and smack 'em good, they're finished. They're hamburger."

Speaking of hamburger, Hawk and Animal have a way of making chopped meat of their opposition. No fancy stuff for these two tough street fighters from the Windy City. No, they are brutally direct. They rely on hard-hitting power tactics such as slams, clotheslines, dropped elbows, hammering forearms, piledrivers, chops — all of which are designed to weaken opponents so Animal can hoist them up on his shoulders and Hawk can trigger the Doomsday Device.

"Let 'em come. Nobody's too big or too fast for the Legion of Doom."

Hawk and Animal are able to use these power tactics so effectively because they both have prodigious strength. They are literally laden with slabs of muscle. They can toss around opponents even larger than they are and do it with astonishing ease.

This same strength enables Hawk and Animal to resist punishment. Lesser opponents seem unable to hurt them. Hawk and Animal can take their blows full force without flinching. Sometimes they even laugh it off. Opponents in their league can hurt the Legion at times, but Hawk and Animal have the ability to weather the storm and come back like thunder and lightning.

More than anything, Hawk and Animal love a good fight. "Bashing heads makes you feel more alive," says Animal. "We don't mind taking a few to give out a few," says Hawk. "Because what we give out is worse than what we take. We're not afraid of anybody. We can whip anybody, anytime."

Indeed, Hawk and Animal have met the best. They crushed the Orient Express and smashed Power and Glory. They stomped on the Nasty Boys and stood tall against the massive Natural Disasters. The fans love it. And they love to see Hawk and Animal come to the ring, wearing their spiked armor, faces painted, scowling, eyes glaring. Come to think of it, they are so scary that many opponents are whipped just by seeing the Legion of Doom stride into the ring. ■

The Warlord

Weight:
320 pounds

From:
Unknown

Birthday:
Unknown

Favorite finishing hold:
The full nelson

Trademark:
Mountainous muscles

Favorite quote:
"I'll break your neck."

Goal:
To win a title by a full nelson submission

. . . .

What a mountain of muscle this wrestler is! The Warlord is as brutal as he is big.

Many observers of the WWF say that, pound for pound, the Warlord has more muscle mass than anyone else in the ring. They are probably right. His chest is huge, his trapezoids stand up like ridges on his shoulders, his neck is like a column and his legs are like oaks. Biceps? His bulge like boulders. No question the Warlord is fearsomely strong. On *WWF Prime Time Wrestling*, he bench-pressed almost 500 pounds 20 times.

The Warlord's wrestling strategy is based purely on his awesome strength. No finely tuned tactics for this brute. He relies on sheer strength with a lot of dirty tricks mixed in.

Most of his tactics rely on pounding with feet, knees, forearms and fists. He also uses high-impact maneuvers, such as bone-crunching powerslams and bearhugs. In the end, however, the Warlord likes to try for his full nelson. Once his fingers are locked behind an opponent's neck, the Warlord can bring to bear all of his might. Relentlessly and ruthlessly he puts on the pressure until his victim is slipping into unconsciousness but still feeling horrendous pain on the vertebrae of the neck. Almost no one caught in the Warlord's full nelson escapes a submission.

One who has escaped, however, is the British Bulldog, who boasts muscles-per-size rivaling those of the Warlord. The Bulldog has bested the Warlord in two major pay-per-view television events, prompting the Warlord to hate him with abiding passion. Others among the Warlord's opponents have paid dearly for his frustration over the Bulldog, as the Warlord has vented his spleen on them.

The Warlord has not suffered his losses well. He tries to dismiss the defeats he has suffered at the hands of the Bulldog. "The referees were biased," says the Warlord. "I know that the Bulldog got favorite treatment from the officials."

Losses to the Bulldog notwithstanding — and, admittedly, the matches were close — the Warlord looms as a force with which to be reckoned in the WWF. Innately ruthless, he has become even more so in recent months. All the while, the Warlord's desire for a title has inflamed him to new heights of cruelty in the ring. He is one big dangerous dude. Anyone who meets him risks painful defeat, if not life and limb. We haven't heard the last from the Warlord. ■

The Warlord's favorite tactic is to batter foes into jelly with powerful blows of his massive arms.

The Natural Disasters

Combined weight:
852 pounds

From:
Earthquake, Canada;
Typhoon, Norfolk,
Virginia

Birthdays:
Earthquake, June 22;
Typhoon, August 5

Favorite finishing hold:
Typhoon splash
followed by Earthquake
vertical splash

Trademark:
Biggest team in the
WWF

Favorite quote:
"Call the Red Cross
because here comes a
disaster."

Goal:
To shake up the WWF

· · · · · · · · · · · · · · · · · · ·

Above: **The
Earthquake vertical
splash.** *Opposite:*
Doing the stomp.

redit skinny Jimmy "Mouth of the South" Hart with managerial genius. In his stable, he had the mighty Earthquake, biggest man in the WWF except Andre the Giant. But out there on the horizon sailed someone who was almost as big and perhaps even stronger — a young behemoth called Tugboat. A one-time friend of Hulk Hogan, Tugboat believed he was headed for glory. But even for a leviathan like Tugboat, glory doesn't come cheap in the WWF. You have to earn it. And that takes time. Probably nobody other than Jimmy Hart recognized that, beneath Tugboat's genial exterior, ambition was diverting his course. Tugboat was ready to take the shortcut. All he needed was someone to point him in the right — or, rather, the wrong — direction. That someone was Jimmy Hart.

Hart got to Tugboat. "Team up with me and Earthquake," he sniveled. "Imagine, the two biggest guys wrestling together on a regular basis in the WWF. You'll be invincible. You'll make money. You'll be feared."

Tugboat pondered. Hart added more fuel to the fire. "Sooner or later you've gotta face Earthquake. It's a natural," Hart oozed. "Somebody could get hurt. Why? Team up, and it'll be great for both of you, baby."

Tugboat did. And changed his name to Typhoon. He and Earthquake became the feared Natural Disasters. These two giants use their monumental size to squash the competition into grease spots. They mangle their opponents with a variety of strongarm maneuvers, including the horrendous double splash. Despite their ponderous size, they manage to tag in and out with surprising speed and coordination. It takes the toughest of the tough, men such as Hawk and Animal of the Legion of Doom, to stand against the thunderous assault of the Natural Disasters.

As if their awesome size were not enough to daunt opponents, the Natural Disasters had at their disposal the canny maneuvers of Jimmy Hart. He is the master of distraction. Yelping, yowling and jabbering into his ever-present megaphone, Hart so disconcerts referees that they cannot concentrate on their job in the ring. However, eventually the Natural Disasters realized that Jimmy "Mouth of the South" Hart was not looking out for their interests. In fact, he was looking out for the interests of Ted DiBiase and IRS. So the Disasters dumped Hart and set out on their own. Good for them! ■

Earthquake and Typhoon

VIRGIL

Weight:
245 pounds

From:
Tennessee

Birthday:
June 14

Favorite finishing hold:
His own modified version of the Million Dollar Dream sleeperhold

Trademark:
A boxing style in the ring

Favorite quote:
"If the right one don't get you, then the left one will."

Goal:
To never again be dependent upon anyone else's money

If ever anyone worked his way from the bottom to the top, it is Virgil. This brawny young wrestler, for reasons beyond his control, hit bottom. Family impoverishment back home sent Virgil seeking a job that would provide enough money to help out his folks. And then, one day, he met the Million Dollar Man Ted DiBiase.

Virgil was a perfect victim for the Million Dollar Man, who likes to use his money to make indigent people crawl. DiBiase hired Virgil as his bodyguard, chauffeur, valet and all-around flunky. Virgil was paid well and was able to help his family. But he paid with his spirit for what DiBiase bought with greenbacks. DiBiase said, "Do," and Virgil did, no matter how demeaning the task. Strolling through one of the ranches that he owns, DiBiase stepped in cow droppings. "Clean off my shoes, Virgil," said DiBiase, and Virgil did.

The abasement carried over into the wrestling ring. DiBiase ordered Virgil to be ready to interfere if the Million Dollar Man was in trouble. It went against Virgil's grain. He had always been an honest guy. But the filthy lucre of the Million Dollar Man was a potent force. Virgil paid again, often with his body, as he was battered on a number of separate occasions by angered DiBiase opponents.

Finally, Virgil realized he was no longer a man but a creature of DiBiase.

Virgil rebelled and, with the support of newfound friend Rowdy Roddy Piper, told DiBiase what to do with his bucks. The Million Dollar Man set out to destroy Virgil. Virgil, in turn, decided to best DiBiase in the ring and take from him his treasured Million Dollar Belt.

Some years back, Virgil had been a boxer. He decided to combine his boxing skills with the wrestling he had learned while with DiBiase. Piper taught him more. At the 1991 *SummerSlam*, Virgil emerged with the victory and the belt.

Later in the year, Virgil and DiBiase met again in the squared circle. This time, DiBiase took the victory and reclaimed the belt, but only with the help of the Repo Man. DiBiase had engaged him to provide assistance. Virgil was disappointed but not discouraged. After all, as a WWF superstar in his own right, he made enough money to continue helping his family. As for the Repo Man, Virgil had a score to settle with him. ■

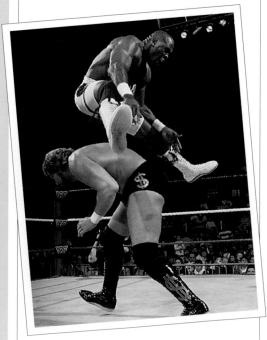

Virgil finally had the chance to meet his former employer in the ring. And Virgil made the best of it, catching DiBiase in Virgil's own Million Dollar Dream.

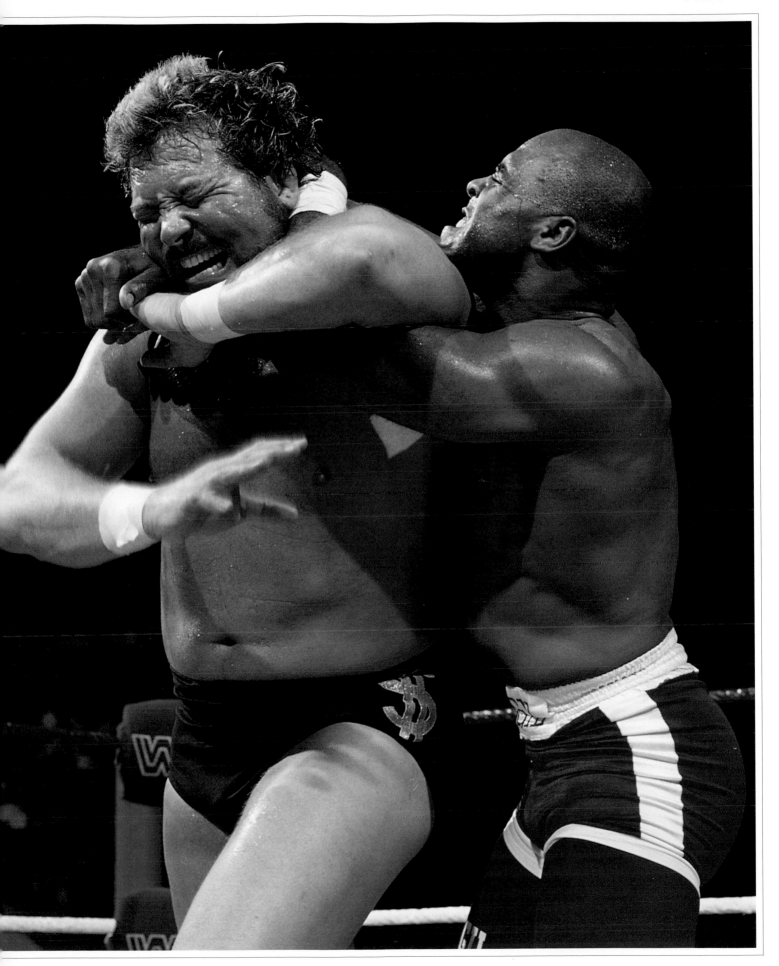

The Bushwhackers

Combined weight:
499 pounds

From:
New Zealand

Birthdays:
Unknown

Favorite finishing hold:
The Bushwhacker battering ram

Trademark:
The Bushwhacker stomp

Favorite quote:
"Bloody lovely — tell your mutha!"

Goal:
To rally all our Bushwhackeroos

They are wild and woolly. They stride about, swinging their arms in the Bushwhacker stomp, mimicked by fans throughout the world.

Their eyes bulge and tongues protrude. They like to lick one another on the head. And they reek of the sardines they so dearly love to gobble by the bucketful. There is no more zany duo in the WWF than the Bushwhackers, the most unorthodox team in WWF tag team ranks.

The Bushwhackers, Luke and Butch, are cousins, hailing from the backwoods of New Zealand. They were reared in the bush, seldom if ever coming in contact with polite society. Perhaps their etiquette leaves something to be desired, but they are genuine nature boys, innocent of cunning, always ready to hold out a hand in friendship. Sometimes it backfires. Luke and Butch took on Tugboat — now Typhoon of the Natural Disasters — as a partner in a six-man tag team match. Their opponents were the Nasty Boys and Earthquake, now the other half of the Disasters. Tugboat turned on the Bushwhackers, threw Butch over the top rope and bigsplashed Luke.

In the long run, it didn't faze the Bushwhackers. They are also tough and durable, a result of their woodsy upbringing. They can both take a battering and dish one out if need be. They took a brutal beating at the hands of the Natural Disasters at *SummerSlam* but nevertheless rebounded to tangle with the Beverly Brothers.

"Yea mates," says Luke. "We know the WWF is a tough place to be. But that's fine for the Bushwhackers because we're tough blokes, you know. Right, Cousin Butch?

"You're on target, Cousin Luke," replies Butch. "Maybe we lost a few,

The Bushwhackers get to work.

but we won a lot, too. And we're not afraid of anybody in the WWF. We showed 'em all."

He's right. Because of their unorthodox style — or lack of any specific style — Luke and Butch are tough nuts for opposing teams to crack. Planning a well-defined strategy against Luke and Butch is next to impossible. When they get on a roll, moreover, look out. The Bushwhackers turn into wild men, slugging and clotheslining with abandon. All in all, one never knows what to expect from the Bushwhackers. That's what makes Luke and Butch one of the most exciting tag teams in the WWF. ■

You've got to love the Bushwhackers! Their antics have earned them the affection of the fans.

"Tell your mutha, we love sardines, we do."

cousins Luke and Butch

Shawn Michaels

Weight:
230 pounds

From:
San Antonio, Texas

Birthday:
July 22

Favorite finishing hold:
Back suplex

Trademark:
Ruthless ambition

Favorite quote:
"You got a problem?"

Goal:
Total glory

Shawn Michaels, managed by Sensational Sherri, has become one of the most cruel and underhanded men in the WWF.

Managed by Sensational Sherri, who can't seem to keep her hands off him, Shawn Michaels is making a reputation for himself as one of the surliest men in the WWF. He has also demonstrated that he is greedy for fame and fortune, so much so that he will use any means at all to win matches.

Moreover, Michaels has shown that he has a monstrous ego. He believes Sherri's contention that he is the world's No.1 sex symbol. Cocky, boastful and totally full of himself, you might think that Michaels would lose touch with what's going on in the ring. On the contrary, he is as gifted a wrestler as he is snotty.

Micheals is an astonishing aerialist, who seems to spend as much time high above the mat as on it. He has a bevy of scientific holds and maneuvers, which he adeptly combines with dirty tricks to attain success.

"WWF Magazine is a yellow rag," says Shawn Michaels. "They don't get anything right. You want proof? They say that Shawn Michaels isn't legit in the ring. I've never broken a rule. Just ask Sherri."

"There's nobody like my Shawn," croons a love-struck Sensational Sherri. Nobody's more handsome. Nobody's built better. And nobody's a better wrestler."

"She's absolutely right," snickers Michaels. "I'm the greatest. I know there are some people out there who say I'm not. But that's just jealousy. They don't bother me. I love to make people jealous. They'll be even more jealous when I have a title." ∎

A member of a legendary wrestling family, brother of the famed Bret "Hit Man" Hart, son of the great Stu Hart, the Rocket Owen Hart is a WWF newcomer who astonishes audiences with his aerial acrobatics. He can use the ropes in many ways as a launching pad, firing him into the air so he can strike with the impact of a missile. Opponents who believe they have tossed him out of the ring find the Rocket flying back at them and landing right on target.

The Rocket, observers believe, is destined for greatness in the WWF. Since entering the WWF's ranks in 1991, he has left a long string of opponents dazzled and confused because of his swift, athletic tactics. Although many of his foes have been larger than he is, they have been unable to corner him in order to use size to their advantage. The Rocket is simply there one moment, gone the next. Adversaries never know from where he will strike next. When he does strike, however, they know it — in spades. ∎

The Rocket Owen Hart

Weight:
225 pounds

From:
Calgary, Alberta, Canada

Birthday:
July 7

Favorite finishing hold:
Rocket launcher splash

Trademark:
Uncanny agility

Favorite quote:
"Rockets away."

Goal:
To keep up the family tradition

The Rocket is an impeccable wrestler and a world-renowned aerialist. Here, he snatches Barry Horowitz in a hammerlock.

Rowdy Roddy Piper

Weight:
234 pounds

From:
Glasgow, Scotland

Birthday:
November 19

Favorite finishing hold:
You name it

Trademark:
His kilt

Favorite quote:
He has a million of them

Goal:
To keep the world wondering about him

His face set with determination, Rowdy Roddy Piper, the flamboyant Scot, makes a ring entrance.

> " I left Glasgow when I was a little, bitty guy, but I always have been proud of my Scottish heritage. It's good to get back there. "

hen they made Rowdy Roddy Piper, they threw away the mold. The ubiquitous Piper — once called "The Man You Love to Hate" — is into everything. He'll step into the ring with anybody at virtually a second's notice. He speaks what is on his mind, no matter whom it offends. As long as he thinks it's right and true, he'll say it. He's starred on television and in motion pictures, including one in which he battled weirdo, goggle-eyed aliens. He's been a stellar WWF announcer. He's gutsy as all get-out, and he plays life to the fullest, always grabbing for the gusto. This native of the United Kingdom is also a wonderfully complex human being who can be warm, caring and totally loyal.

Piper's humane side was evident when he helped rescue Virgil from the clutches of the Million Dollar Man Ted DiBiase, earning DiBiase's undying enmity. His rugged side is evident from the fierce opponents whom, over the years, he has met head-on, often in spectaculars such as *Wrestle-Mania* and the *Survivor Series*. Hulk Hogan, Mr. T, the late Adrian Adonis, Ravishing Rick Rude, Bad News Brown, Mr. Perfect, IRS, DiBiase and Ric Flair are just a few of the rugged individuals with whom Piper has traded blows.

"Right on, bubba," says Piper. "I don't care whom I get into the ring with. The tougher the better. It keeps old Hot Rod's life from getting boring. You know, I've got to keep moving, don't I? All work and no play makes Roddy a dull boy."

Dull Piper will never be. He is always there with the unexpected, whether it's an outrageous observation or a lightning bodyslam.

Piper is a study in contrasts. He teased and chided Macho Man Randy Savage, who spent time in the WWF television announcer's booth with him. And yet when Savage and his bride Elizabeth were menaced by the

The Million Dollar Man Ted DiBiase's face is about to impact on a ring turnbuckle, courtesy of Rowdy Roddy Piper.

evil Jake "The Snake" Roberts, Piper put himself on the line to help Savage.

Like the British Bulldog, Scotsman Piper is happy about the increasing popularity of the WWF in the UK. ■

The Berzerker

Weight:
322 pounds

From:
Iceland

Birthday:
Unknown

Favorite finishing hold:
Prefers throwing opponent out of the ring for count-out

Trademark:
Horned helmet, shield and sword

Favorite quote:
"Huss...Husss..." (whatever that means)

Goal:
To pillage the WWF

....

Mr. Fuji's Berzerker, the wild Northman, mauls an opponent at his manager's command.

In the early Middle Ages, people in England, France and other European countries lived in fear of Viking raids. They prayed, "Deliver us, Lord, from the fury of the Northman." The most frenzied fighters among the Vikings, or Northmen, were berserkers. Wild-eyed and battle-crazed, they feared nothing, seeking only the destruction of their foe.

The foes of the Berzerker in the WWF know about the fury of this giant Northman. Coached by his manager, Mr. Fuji, the Berzerker rampages over his opponents with wild abandon. Kicks, hammering chops and illegal closed-hand blows are among his favorite weapons.

The only force in the world that seems able to control the fury of the Berzerker is a telepathic signal from Mr. Fuji, or so he claims. The method, Fuji says, is mind-to-mind manipulation. Here's how it works. When Fuji clutches his wrist, the signal is transmitted to the Berzerker. Fuji asserts that in this manner he can channel the destructive energies of the Berzerker in whatever way he sees fit.

Like the Vikings of old, the Berzerker has left a trail of beaten and broken bodies in his wake. Where that trail will eventually lead this ferocious Northman is anyone's guess. It is certain, however, that plenty more carnage is in store along the way. ■

lad in a top hat and waving a skull with smoke emanating from the eye sockets, Papa Shango is an intimidating sight. His face is painted white, save for a black spot on the tip of his nose, matching circles around the eyes and two red bars on his cheeks. He is the voodoo man of the WWF, a fearsome ogre who claims he can use black magic to destroy his enemies.

"Chango" — a variation of his name — is known as the voodoo god of power, passion and control of enemies. It's no wonder that Papa Shango chose his name.

"I will control all who try to oppose me," says Papa Shango, with a look of particularly savage evil on his grotesque face. I will show them the power of my dark magic."

Shango's rituals stem from voodoo, brought to Haiti by slaves from West Africa. His supporters attend all his matches. As he enters the arena, their hands begin to drum on their seats as they beg the spirits to support him. It must work because he appears to be indestructible. ∎

Weight:
325 pounds

From:
Unknown

Birthday:
Unknown

Favorite finishing hold:
A variety of power moves

Trademark:
Bizarre voodoo garb

Favorite quote:
"It is the night of blood, Ybo."

Goal:
To cast a spell on the WWF

. . . .

After he defeats his opponent, Papa Shango performs a voodoo ceremony to ensure the wrestler's soul suffers as much as his body.

Hacksaw Jim Duggan

Weight:
280 pounds

From:
Glens Falls, New York

Birthday:
January 14

Favorite finishing hold:
Running clothesline

Trademark:
His two-by-four, American flag and patriotism

Favorite quote:
"God bless America."

Goal:
To always stand by the USA

Hacksaw Jim Duggan is something else again. This burly but good-natured brawler is as rough-hewn as the timber that is taken from the forests of his native upstate New York. He is as rugged as the Adirondack Mountains of the same region. He's a smalltown boy with a very big frame — and a huge heart, to boot. Above all, Hacksaw Jim Duggan is a patriot, proud of the USA and all its allies.

Fans adore him because, despite his great success in the wrestling ring, he has never forgotten he is just a common working man. He identifies with the men and women who roll up their sleeves in industry and agriculture, who build roads and erect buildings. There is nothing stuffy about Hacksaw Jim Duggan and nothing complicated either.

"I'm a simple guy with simple values," he says. "I know right from wrong, and that's all you have to know. I'm for my country and my countrymen — and anybody who stands with them. That's the way I live. You don't have to go about making life complicated."

But Hacksaw does make life complicated for his opponents in the ring. His wrestling style is like his lifestyle — direct, powerful and uncomplicated. Power moves, basic and direct, are his forte. The worst thing an opponent can try is to duke it out with him. Then Hacksaw is in his glory. There is nothing he likes better than a free-for-all with someone who tries to get down and dirty. When it comes to flying fists, Hacksaw can be a genuine

terror. Riled up, he seems to be almost impervious to pain.

During the fall of 1991, Hacksaw found himself a new ally in another patriot, one who had forsaken his country and then returned to it. That man is Sgt. Slaughter. He and Hacksaw are cut from the same cloth. Both would do anything in defense of their

Above: Hacksaw Jim Duggan carries Old Glory proudly. **Opposite:** He is always ready to put his trusty two-by-four to good use.

flag, their land and freedom. Hacksaw, of course, never wavered the way Slaughter did when he formed an alliance with the tyrannical General Adnan and Colonel Mustafa. However, Hacksaw doesn't hold this unfortunate act against Slaughter.

"It takes lots of guts to admit you're wrong. Sarge and I are tougher. If anybody doesn't like it, too bad, Tough Guy. Hoooo." ■

Take this big "Hoooooo," howls Hacksaw Jim Duggan, as he brandishes his two-by-four.

El Matador

Weight:
244 pounds

From:
Tocula, Mexico

Birthday:
May 10

Favorite finishing hold:
El Paseo del Muerte and flying forearm

Trademark:
His suit of lights

Favorite quote:
"Toro"

Goal:
To face the fiercest bulls in the wrestling ring

El Matador makes it rough on an opponent. Tito Santana became El Matador when he rediscovered his Hispanic roots.

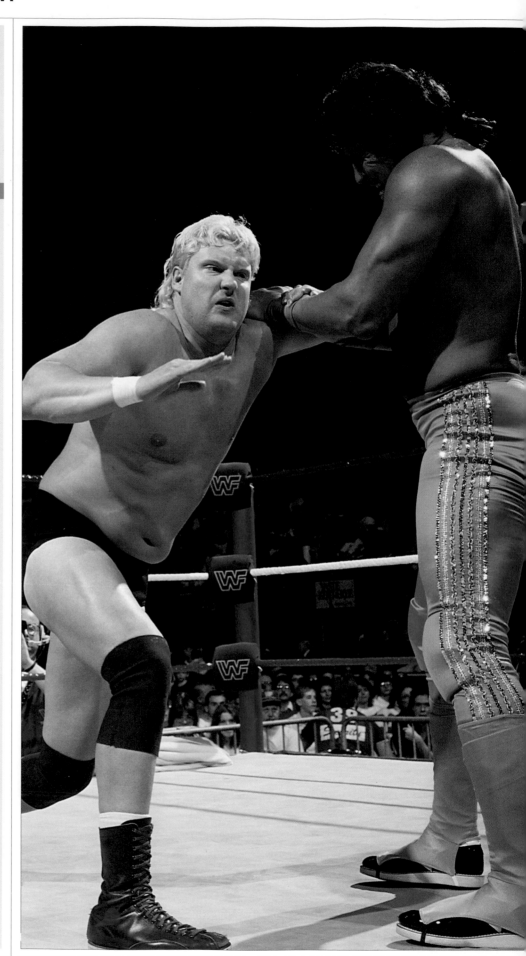

While Tito Santana was growing up in his hometown of Tocula, Mexico, he would often go with his family to Mexico City and visit the arena where matadors would challenge the fighting bulls. Young Tito marveled at the courage and agile grace of the matadors and wished that he could be one of them. Today, he is.

As Tito matured, however, his dreams of entering the bull ring took second place to the realities of life: school, athletics and finally the need to earn a living. Tito took his athleticism to the wrestling ring and eventually joined the WWF, where he became an established star, even an Intercontinental Champion.

Over the years, Santana distinguished himself as a successful veteran of the squared circle, a consistent winner, fiery yet not flamboyant. A time came, however, when he began to question himself. The fire was dying. Despite his continued successes in the squared circle, something was missing.

Santana did some self-searching. He remembered his Hispanic roots and the matadors he had admired as a boy. The matador is the ultimate hero of Hispanic tradition. Tito decided to become a matador. Off he went to Mexico and enrolled in a school for men who want to face the bulls.

"It wasn't a hasty decision. I knew I could be hurt, but that can happen in the wrestling ring as well as in the bull ring. I had to do it, so I did."

Returning as El Matador, clad in the matador's "suit of lights," Tito stunned opponents by combining the tactics of the wrestling ring with those of the bull ring. Since then, foes have been awed by his Paseo del Muerte, the move the matador makes before placing his sword into the bull. In Tito's case, however, it is not a sword but a flying forearm off the ropes that puts his opponent down. ∎

Viva El Matador! He is resplendent in his "suit of lights," the traditional costume of the matador. El Matador shines in the ring as well.

Repo Man

Weight:
286 pounds

From:
Detroit, Michigan

Birthday:
April 1

Favorite finishing hold:
The Crowbar

Trademark:
Hanging defeated opponents from the ropes by his tow rope

Favorite quote:
"What's mine is mine. What's yours is mine, too."

Goal:
To repossess every belt in the WWF

Repo Man ties up a defeated opponent prior to hauling him to the ropes. Repo is the ultimate thief in the night.

In the dark of night lurks Repo Man, ready to repossess anything you own. If you are a day late on your car payments, he's after your vehicle. Forget to send in the credit card payment on the new TV? One night when you're asleep, Repo Man will get it. When the economy is bad, Repo Man enjoys life more. The reason? There are more items to repossess.

"What's mine is mine," he snickers. "What's yours is mine, too."

Repo Man has promised his opponents in the WWF he will repossess any claims they have to fame, any victories. He did it to Virgil who had beaten the Million Dollar Man Ted DiBiase fair and square and taken his Million Dollar Belt. In a rematch, Repo Man, engaged by DiBiase, repossessed the belt and helped DiBiase defeat his former bodyguard.

Sneaky and mean as he is, Repo Man is very good at what he does, within the squared circle as well as out of it. He kicks in opponents' ribs as savagely as he kicks in the windows of automobiles he is out to repossess. He sneaks around the ring with the same stealth with which he creeps into homes to remove furniture. His future opponents best keep a keen eye out for Repo Man. ■

Hercules

Weight:
275 pounds

From:
Tampa, Florida

Birthday:
May 7

Favorite finishing hold:
The backbreaker

Trademark:
A steel chain

Favorite quote:
"I am the mighty Hercules."

Goal:
To put all my opponents in chains

Hercules tries a test of strength with Rowdy Roddy Piper and attempts to power him to the canvas.

In the past, Hercules has claimed to be the modern-day version of the legendary Greek hero of the same name, the strongest man in the world. Whether or not you believe Hercules, he does. That gives him a very positive mind-set when he enters the squared circle. He believes he is invincible, and that helps him win matches. When he loses a match, he tells himself that outside forces — a referee's prejudice, for example — were responsible.

Hercules is a rugged individual, so intent on victory that he will use any means to get it. He believes that the strong should own the world. Thus, if he finds he cannot outwrestle an opponent by legitimate means, he tries to use his strength to injure his foe. And he has strength aplenty. His body is awesome. Muscles bulge on muscles. Sinews ripple like steel cords. His body looks as hard as the marble statues in Greek temples.

During the heat of a hard-fought match, Hercules can erupt into a frightening rage. He grits his teeth, knots his fists and his eyes bulge from their sockets, glaring with fury. Observers wonder whether this is instinctive behavior or a psychological ploy to cow his opponents. Either way, it often works for Hercules. ■

The Model Rick Martel

Weight:
242 pounds

From:
Cocoa Beach, Florida

Birthday:
August 27

Favorite finishing hold:
Boston crab

Trademark:
Arrogance

Favorite quote:
"I am the Model"

Goal:
To continue to be the best-dressed man in the world

Nose in the air, a smirk on his face, the Model Rick Martel is the essence of arrogance. In fact, his favorite cologne is called "Arrogance." It's not a favorite of his opponents. "Arrogance," which Martel carries in a sprayer, contains an ingredient extremely irritating to the eyes. And the Model is fond of spraying it into the eyes of his adversaries.

Martel believes he is the world's fashion leader. He swaggers around in high-fashion garb he selects from leading designers around the globe. Every so often, he travels the world, studying fashions and obtaining what he feels are the latest and most elegant of threads.

> "The WWF is lucky to have the Model in its ranks. I lend the WWF a sense of elegance and class."

The Model says that he is such a gorgeous person that he makes the finest clothing look even better. "Look

at this magnificent body of mine and all its finely sculpted muscles," he says. "Examine my handsome face, my pearly smile. I was born to wear the most elegant clothes possible."

Indeed, for all his boasting, the Model has a point. He is a superb physical specimen, and although we hate to admit it, he is undeniably handsome. He also is a highly accomplished wrestler who has mastered myriad moves and holds, and he blends strength with speed and agility. Coupled with his athletic prowess is an ability to use dirty tricks and get away with it. The Model is a master sneak, able to pull off cheap shots without being caught very often by the referee.

The hold that the Model loves most is his feared Boston crab. Once he cinches it in, few opponents can escape. Bending back his face-down victim's legs in a painful arch, the Model puts on the pressure. Braced on his own legs, he puts such muscle and weight into the hold that the pain it causes is excruciating. And that's just the way the Model likes it. Even after he gains a submission, he is likely to keep on the pressure and the hurt until the referee forces him to release the hold.

"Many of my opponents need to be taught an extra lesson," says the Model by way of explanation for his excessive brutality. "I just keep them in the Boston crab for a little while longer so they know they have been foolish to try to compete with the Model." ∎

Left: In late 1990, the Model Rick Martel developed a cologne known as Arrogance. **Right:** The Model ensnares an adversary in the Boston crab — Martel's finisher.

Combined weight:
546 pounds

From:
Allentown,
Pennsylvania

Birthdays:
Knobbs, May 6; Sags,
July 5

Favorite finishing hold:
Knobbs powerslam,
followed by Sags elbow
off the top turnbuckle

Trademark:
Crude behavior

Favorite quote:
"We're gonna Nastisize
you."

Goal:
To stomp the world
under our boots

The Nasty Boys have faces so ugly that when they were born their mothers tried to give them back. True or not, that's what the Nastys are fond of claiming. They rejoice in their ugliness, their crude behavior and, especially, in stomping on people. If any two wrestlers in the WWF are truly down and dirty, they are the Nasty Boys, who are managed by Jimmy "Mouth of the South" Hart. Even the most ruthless tag teams have at least a few qualities that are to be admired, if not respected. The Nasty Boys have

none. What is more, they are proud of their reputation.

They are just what their team name implies — pure nastiness.

The Nasty Boys were in the WWF only a few months when they won a tag team tournament to decide who would face the then-titlists at the time, the Hart Foundation, at *WrestleMania VII*. They defeated the Foundation, but only through skulduggery, at which they excel. As WWF Tag Team Champions, they continued the reign of terror they had begun the first time they stepped into the ring. Gouging,

Knobbs and Sags

kicking and punching, they are the street thugs of the WWF.

"We get our jollies in only one way," says Knobbs. "That's terrorizing the guts out of people."

"Anybody who gets up close and personal with the Nasty Boys is gonna end up with our boot prints all over his body," says Sags.

All the nastiness in the world, however, couldn't save the Nasty Boys from losing the title at *SummerSlam*. The Legion of Doom, Hawk and Animal, gave the Nastys a dose of their own medicine — bare-knuckle street fighting. Losing the title hurt the Nasty Boys but, in the long run, has hurt their opponents more. Since *WrestleMania VII*, the Nasty Boys have been even more brutal and vicious than before. They have been venting their spleen on everyone they meet in the squared circle. Typically, a battered and defeated opponent is likely to have his face shoved into a stinking Nasty armpit or a dirty Nasty toe shoved into his mouth. Often, however, the opponent is so out of it he hardly knows what is happening, which is probably better for him. ∎

The Nasty Boys are just that: nasty. They are basically thugs who bring their vicious behavior into the ring.

....

Skinner

Weight:
235 pounds

From:
The Florida Everglades

Birthday:
November 22

Favorite finishing hold:
Gatorbreaker

Trademark:
Spitting tobacco juice

Favorite quote:
"I'm gonna skin you alive."

Goal:
To tack all my opponents' hides on the wall

There's an old song by the Everly Brothers that talks of "running like a dog through the Everglades." That dog was probably running from Skinner. This backwoods bully, who looks as if the only time he bathes is when he falls into a slough, is the terror of the swamps. Skinner was raised in the most remote 'Glades of Collier County. People down there say he was born on a cypress head, surrounded by alligators, panthers and cottonmouths. They say he never left the 'Glades until he was 20 years old. He is totally at home amid the sawgrass, gator holes and live oaks.

Skinner is savage, but there's nothing noble about it. He wears his clothes until they rot off his back. Tobacco juice drools from his lips — juice that he enjoys spattering upon a fallen foe. He is truly gross.

Starting as a young boy, Skinner has haunted the 'Glades, skinning knife in hand, seeking animal prey. He is not a sportsman who hunts and traps by the rules and looks for a clean kill. No, Skinner is an extremely cruel man who enjoys inflicting cruelty upon animals — and upon his opponents in the ring.

"Anybody who messes with old Skinner, here," says he while biting off a chaw, "is gonna get skinned alive and have his hide handed to him. Skinner, he's gonna stalk through the WWF just the way he does in the 'Glades back home. And he's gonna track down his victims, and then he's gonna tan their hides."

Skinner's words are a good description of his ring style. He stalks his foe with a swamper's craft, not closing in until he senses the time is ripe for the kill. Skinner doesn't like to tangle until he is absolutely certain that the advantages are all his. Then he rips into the adversary with an ugly assortment of illegal tactics.

Just as Skinner camouflages himself while in the boonies, he masks his

Above: Skinner does some face mashing. *Opposite:* Here Skinner tries some rough stuff on El Matador.

intentions in the ring. Although crude and seemingly dull of wit, he is a master of deception. "I'm just like a mean old bull gator," he says. "He lays there in the water, with just his eyes above the surface, looking like a dirty old log. But when some critter he likes to eat comes close enough to him, he makes his move real fast, opens up those jaws — and goodbye critter. That's just like Skinner." ∎

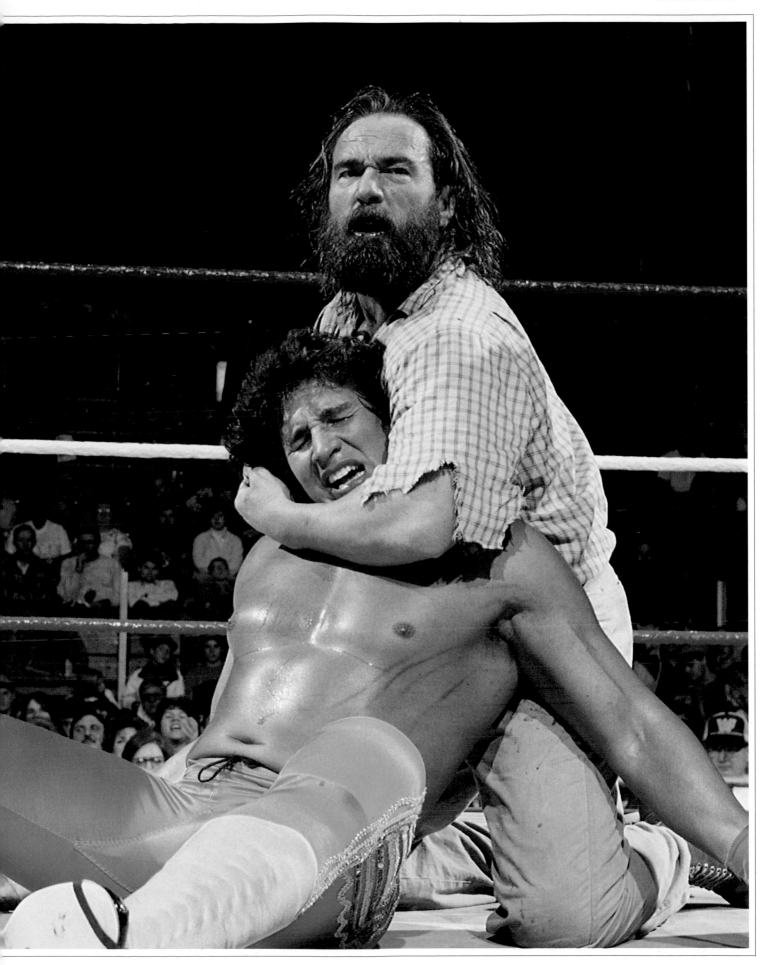

Tatanka

Weight:
235 pounds

From:
Pembroke, North Carolina

Birthday:
March 21

Favorite finishing hold:
He is developing a series of new holds

Trademark:
Tremendous pride in his Native American heritage

Favorite quote:
"I will soar like an eagle in the WWF."

Tatanka, once known as Chris Chavis, is an example of a young man who has returned to his roots and been reborn. Tatanka is a member of the Lumbee tribe of Native Americans, residents of North Carolina. As a student he excelled in both academics and athletics. He was an honor student and an All-American gridiron star. He then took his athleticism to the wrestling ring where he was — and is — viewed as one of the most promising young matmen in years.

Despite his many accomplishments, Chavis wasn't at peace with himself. "I knew that somehow I wasn't whole," says Tatanka, remembering. "But I wasn't sure why."

He found out one night back in North Carolina when he visited his people. In the dark of night by a blazing campfire, he sat while the Lumbees danced in a joyous celebration, exulting in the Native American heritage of which they are so proud. As the drums pounded, echoing in the darkness, and the bells on the dancers tinkled, he suddenly realized what was missing from his life.

"I had not discovered my true roots," says Tatanka. "Or at least I had not realized how much the importance of being a Native American was to my life. The drums told me. The expressions on the faces of the dancers told me. I had to steep

> ### "I pledge that I will restore the ethics and traditions of Native Americans to their rightful place."

myself in my Indian heritage."

So the young man, with the help of a revered shaman, underwent a purification ceremony. And he began to grow spiritually. Today Tatanka is the leader of the New Indian Nation — and a wrestler who will indeed soar like an eagle. ∎

Tatanka grabs an opponent in a headlock.

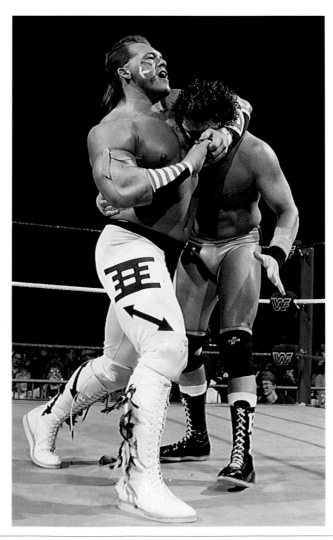

The story of Brutus "The Barber" Beefcake is one of tragedy and triumph. Brutus, who once wore a WWF Tag Team Championship Belt, was one of the most successful and idolized wrestlers in the squared circle. Zany and colorful, given to clipping the hair of defeated opponents, Brutus also was one of the best-liked of all of the WWF athletes.

Then, in 1990 during the July 4 holiday weekend, a tragedy occurred. Brutus was horribly injured in a parasailing accident in Tampa, Florida. The Barber collided with another parasailer in midair, shattering most of the bones in his face. Rushed to a hospital's intensive care unit, Brutus was examined by physicians, who said it appeared as if his face was collapsing under its own weight.

During nine hours of surgery, doctors implanted eight steel plates — held together by 24 screws and bone taken from Brutus' skull — inside his face. When he awoke after surgery, Brutus looked into the mirror and saw an old friend looking back. His face was unmarred by stitches. Subsequently, Brutus made a remarkable recovery, a triumph of perseverance and courage. Within a month after his release from the hospital, he was lifting weights once again.

"Now," says Brutus, "I'm back in the World Wrestling Federation I'm real happy and grateful, because I wouldn't have made it back without the support of my fans." ∎

Weight:
271 pounds

From:
San Francisco, California

Birthday:
April 21

Trademark:
Clipping hair with his shears

Favorite quote:
"I think I'll snip a little more off over the ears."

Goal:
To keep struttin' and cuttin' in the WWF

Brutus "The Barber" Beefcake

. . . .

Watch out, you're gonna get clipped. Brutus "The Barber" Beefcake is a fast man with his shears.

NO HOLDS BARRED

Wristlocks, clotheslines, snapmares and bodyslams rarely win matches — a possible exception would be the British Bulldog's devastating powerslam — but they do soften up an opponent for the stunning finisher.

espite the fact that Jake "The Snake" Roberts is one of the most despised men in wrestling today, a look at his arsenal is a view of a winning formula. Perhaps more than anyone else in the WWF, Roberts knows how to best combine psychology with technical mat work and brawling tactics. He never wrestles the same in any two matches and thus constantly keeps his foes guessing. In one contest, he can be absolutely demonic, attacking a man before the bell and battering him mercilessly. The next night he may shock an opponent by coming at him with not a fist or a boot but a scientific leg dive followed by a fireman's carry and hammerlock, all a prelude to the same finish — the brutal DDT.

In order to apply the DDT, Jake must first trap his opponent in a front facelock, then drive his head into the mat. From someone watching in the third or fourth row, this seems like an easy move to apply. However, Roberts must rely on his mat sense — acquired over years in the squared circle — to determine whether his rival is sufficiently weakened or whether he's still strong enough to block the finisher.

"Some people have told me that matches are won and lost through heart," Jake says, smiling mysteriously. "I beg to differ. When you look at Jake 'The Snake' Roberts, you're looking at a man with a heart as dark as the blackest coal from the deepest depths of the earth. So I'd have to say my formula for success is

Jake "The Snake" Roberts is the master of the DDT. This skullcrusher has sent many of Jake's opponents straight to la-la land.

something more primitive — the same as an animal that senses a vulnerability in its quarry and knows it's time to swallow it up."

Often, Roberts prepares his opponent for the DDT with a clothesline — not the monstrous clotheslines delivered by powerhouses like Hulk Hogan, Undertaker, Sid Justice and Big Boss Man — but a crafty variation that can only be described as reptilian in nature. To increase impact, Roberts actually whips his foe into the clothesline, grabbing him in a wristlock, then slinging him backward and arching him forward into an extended arm. By delivering this short-arm clothesline at such close range, Jake can do more damage than his heavier colleagues who do not hold on to their opponents when utilizing the move.

Jake the Snake clamps a sleeperhold on Macho Man Randy Savage to soften him up for an application of the dreaded DDT and bring about a hoped-for victory.

....

In reality, Jake's intuition comes from being in the heat of the mat wars for a sizable chunk of his controversial life and knowing how effective his run-of-the-mill maneuvers are.

Another remarkable athlete who has his foes all but terminated by the time the finisher is applied is Bret "Hit Man" Hart. Like Jake, the second-generation dynamo is as equally adept at fisticuffs as he is at exchanging technical holds on the mat. Also, Hart is an excellent defensive wrestler, able to wiggle out of maneuvers and bridge out of near-falls. Throughout the course of a match, Bret methodically wears his man down, then puts him away with the sharpshooter, bending his opponent in a Boston crab variation on the mat and administering a painful leg grapevine simultaneously.

Shawn Michaels expends just as much sweat and toil, but much of it is in the air. He can get free from a wristlock by leaping up, sling-shotting himself off the ropes, spinning in midair and setting his adversary up for one of the dozens of aerial moves he applies.

Remarkably, Million Dollar Man Ted DiBiase is also fleet-footed, although his obnoxious boasts tend to cloud his talent. Between the ropes, DiBiase is a master at side-stepping stampeding foes and firing back with fists and punches. Once his opponent is on the canvas, the Million Dollar Man may batter him

The Million Dollar Man Ted DiBiase uses his Million Dollar Dream sleeperhold with lethal effectiveness. Here an opponent goes beddy-bye.

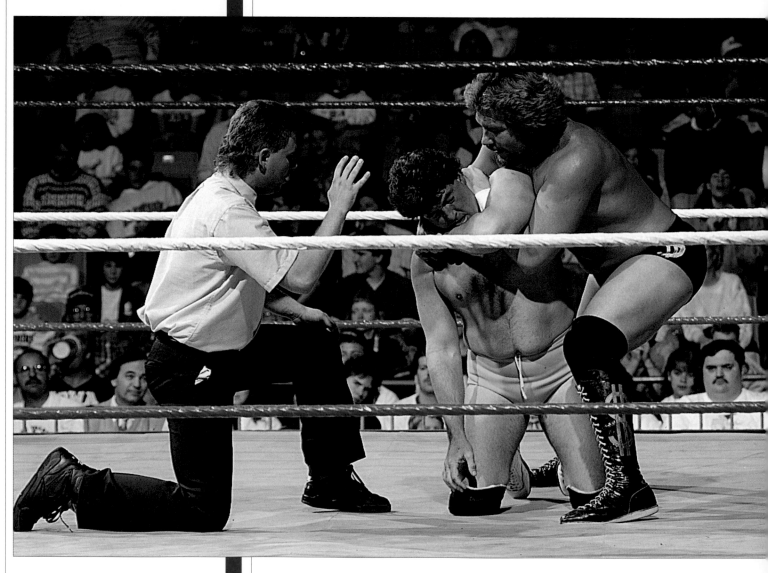

with kicks to the side of the head, debilitate him with suplexes and snapmares or outwrestle him with a spinning toe hold — an agonizing, classic submission maneuver. Ultimately, his rival is likely to find himself in the Million Dollar Dream, a form of the sleeperhold that almost always saps the victim's consciousness and brings the crass moneyman a ring victory.

One of the few competitors to have logged a victory over the Million Dollar Man is Macho Man Randy Savage, a wrestler of similar size and experience. It was DiBiase whom Macho Man defeated in the final round of a tournament to become the World Wrestling Federation Champion in 1988, and — although allies of both men interfered in the contest — most mat experts agree that Savage outwrestled his foe.

What makes Randy's stockpile of maneuvers particularly dangerous is his brutality. He may throw a foe over the top rope, then climb the turnbuckles and smash him on the arena floor with a double axhandle.

Savage can leave his feet quickly and come down on his opponent with any number of injurious moves.

When it's time to call it a night, Savage pummels his adversary until he is flat on the mat. Then the Macho Man scales the ropes, soars up toward the arena lights, crooks his arm and blasts his prey with a stunning elbow to the chest or the throat. "Oooh yeaa, the flying elbow's been good to me, just like a loyal old friend," Savage comments. "But I'm gonna let you in on a little personal secret: If I don't execute it at precisely the right moment, it could be curtains for the Macho Man. All a guy has to do is roll out of the way — and it's happened way more times than I'd like to remember — and the Macho Man goes crashing into the ring without even a net to break his fall. At the same time, if he doesn't have the strength to get out of the way, there's nowhere to run and nowhere to hide."

Like a missile, Macho Man Randy Savage strikes from the top turnbuckle with a devastating double axhandle, one of his trademarks.

El Matador's flying dropkick puts him right up there with the aerialists of the WWF. And that's no bull.

••••••••••••••••••••••••••••••••

"If Mexico's air force could do the same things El Matador does when he leaves the ground," Savage observes, "that country would be a world power."

Before he was WWF Champion, Savage held the Intercontinental Belt — a title he won from El Matador Tito Santana. To this day, Savage maintains tremendous respect for El Matador, which is based on the handsome Mexican's airborne wrestling style.

Many in wrestling agree that El Matador possesses one of the most destructive dropkicks in wrestling. This has much to do with the former Intercontinental titlist's timing: As his opponent moves toward him,

Santana does not rush, but rather waits until the man is in perfect position to be zapped.

After a series of dropkicks, Matador is ready to execute his prized finisher — El Paseo de Muerte. Literally translated from Spanish, this means "the pass of death" and is a popular bullfighting term. The well-liked Latino will frequently Irish-whip his foe and — as the man rebounds back — assault him with this adaptation of a flying elbow. At impact, Santana brings one fist down onto his opponent's back, like a matador thrusting a sword into a charging bull.

From time to time, El Matador scores a win with a figure-four leglock. While most of his colleagues openly concede that they'd hate to be trapped in Santana's rendition of this hold — which applies stress to seven separate portions of the body — the true wizard of the figure-four is generally considered to be the owner of the WWF Championship title, Ric Flair.

Flair uses several tactics in order to set up his opponent for the figure-four leglock. However, he is most likely to use it after he disables his adversaries through a combination of hard chops, vicious suplexes and underhanded tactics outside the squared circle.

The larger a wrestler is, the easier it is for him to plow over an opponent with a high-momentum move. To smaller competitors, a shoulderblock is frequently a maneuver delivered at the beginning of a match, when both wrestlers are feeling each other out. The barrel-chested Hacksaw Jim Duggan, on the other hand, has refined his own type of shoulderblock and made it into a finisher. From his days of playing American football, Duggan became adept at the flying tackle, which involves planting your feet firmly on the canvas with your shoulder jutting out in front of you and your fingers on the ground, while holding your body in position. When the victim is in your sights, you charge forward like a defensive end on the Dallas Cowboys, leaving your feet and propelling your shoulder into your adversary, forcing him onto the mat for a pinfall.

Hacksaw Jim Duggan prepares to launch his shoulderblock — the maneuver he has developed into a finisher.

The Undertaker's Tombstone, really a reverse piledriver.

Wham! When the great Hulk Hogan lets go with his patented big boot to the kisser, opponents go down.

Another power-move maven is the Big Boss Man. Perhaps more than any other wrestler of his massive dimensions, he can move as swiftly as a man nearly 100 pounds lighter. Yet, when he decides to slow down and go blow-for-blow, it's nearly impossible to match his might.

"Being suplexed by the Big Boss Man is one experience I wouldn't want anyone else to endure," says a former opponent. "When he locks you up in that double underhook before he actually takes you up into the air, there's no chance of breaking free. Also, because of his enormity, it's next to impossible to shift your weight and reverse the move."

The former Georgia corrections officer's signature maneuver is his spike-slam, also dubbed the Boss Man Slam. He'll sling an opponent into the ropes, sidestep the man as he bounces back toward the center of the ring, then grip him around the waist, take him off the ground and slam him into the canvas.

No one is shocked by the fact that former WWF Champion the Undertaker is also pretty good about beating men into the mat. What is astonishing is the macabre wrestler's ability to move swiftly, ducking under clotheslines, hurling himself at opponents with shoulderblocks and blocking quick-flying punches and kicks. All of that appears to be overshadowed by his ghastly obsession with the world beyond. His grizzly rhetoric notwithstanding, few fans can erase the dreadful memory of witnessing the Undertaker's tombstone, a reverse piledriver responsible for sending many athletes to the emergency room.

His victim list is impressive, and Hulk Hogan is at the top of it. Hogan was injured at the *Survivor Series* in 1991 when Ric Flair slid a chair under the ropes and Undertaker tombstoned the Hulkster on top of it. But, relying on what he has termed the "positive vibrations" of his Hulkamaniacs, Hogan recovered quickly and defeated the Undertaker in a rematch several days later.

BOOT TO THE FACE

The Hulkamaniacs' energy plays a large role in Hogan's offense. But the Hulkster's numerous other attributes include his strength — he's one of the few men to ever bodyslam seven-foot-five-inch Andre the Giant — and a decapitating clothesline. He also uses a damaging "big foot" — executed when he whips a man into the ropes and greets him with a boot to the face — and the legdrop that is responsible for some of his greatest conquests in the ring.

When it comes to tag teaming, the entire concept of holds and finishes becomes more complex. No longer is a win an individual achievement — it's a dual effort. The Beverly Brothers' Shaker Heights Spike — when one Beverly hoists the foe into the air and the other runs his face into the mat — and the Legion of Doom's Doomsday Device — in which the victim sits on Animal's shoulders and Hawk comes off the top rope with a clothesline — are examples of some of the most productive team finishers. But none of these spectacular maneuvers would be possible if the wrestlers hadn't first educated themselves in the fundamentals of the squared circle. ■

WWF

Hawk scores with the Doomsday Device, felling an opponent who is trapped on partner Animal's shoulders.

66 Not many people
get up after
the Boss Man
Slam, brother. 99
HULK HOGAN

With the exception of Elizabeth, the sensitive and beautiful bride of Macho Man Randy Savage, the managers of the WWF are a rather unsavory lot, wheelers and dealers all.

THE MANAGERS OF WWF

They incessantly argue over which of them is the best manager in the WWF, a question that has gone unanswered and probably always will.

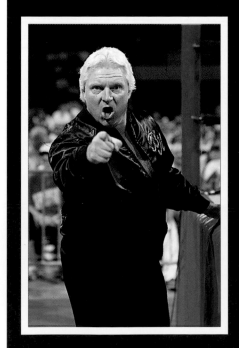

Elizabeth

From:
Sarasota, Florida

Birthday:
November 19

Managerial style:
Inspires and gives courage and loyalty

Favorite quote:
"Oh yeaaa." (Her response to Macho Man's proposal of marriage)

Goal:
Being the best wife possible to the Macho Man

Elizabeth, the lovely "First Lady of the WWF," is more than a manager to Macho Man Randy Savage. She is his wife. After a period of estrangement that began when Mega-Powers Hulk Hogan and Savage split up, Elizabeth and Randy were married in the ring at *Summer-Slam*. The wedding, proclaimed a "Match Made in Heaven," was seen by millions of people worldwide on television.

"It was the most wonderful moment of my life," says Elizabeth. "I dreamed it would happen, but many times I thought it never would. When we were finally married, I could hardly believe it. I was incredibly happy."

Hours later, however, Elizabeth's joy turned to horror as Jake "The Snake" Roberts interrupted the wedding reception. Uninvited, he menaced Elizabeth with a snake. The episode is described elsewhere in this book, in sections dealing with Savage, the Snake and *SummerSlam*.

Jake was not finished. He began a campaign of terror against Savage and Elizabeth, going so far as to manhandle her in the ring in front of a television audience numbering in the millions. Assaulted psychologically and physically by Jake, fearing for her husband's well-being, Elizabeth's wedded bliss turned into a nightmare. Even so, she did not break. Typically, she faced adversity and danger with quiet courage, never for an instant putting her own welfare above that of her man.

Elizabeth's bravery and steadfast support of the Macho Man have earned this slender, gentle beauty the respect of some of the most rugged men in the world, including such WWF superstars as Hulk Hogan.

"She's always ready with a nice word," says the young WWF star Tatanka. "Elizabeth is the salt of the earth. I have great admiration for her. She's kind and caring. I think she

Elizabeth was first the manager of Macho Man Randy Savage and then his wife. Her quiet strength helps steel him for the ring.

gives Macho Man Randy Savage a spiritual strength that helps carry him through difficult times."

Asked what he loved most about Elizabeth, her talkative husband, the Macho Man, was for once at a loss for words. Finally, he furrowed his brow and thought about it for a while. You could tell his mind was hard at work. Suddenly his face grew red and intense, and he exploded with one word — "Everything." ■

"In her own quiet way," says the Hulkster, "Elizabeth is a tower of strength. It's a strength that goes far beyond physical power. It's spiritual strength. You can't develop that kind of strength by pumping iron. Either you're born with it or you're not."

> Lots of people owe me big-time.

Bobby "The Brain" Heenan, that slippery fellow from Beverly Hills, now fancies himself more a "broadcast journalist" than a WWF manager. That may be, but as a manager he piloted some of the most successful wrestlers in the WWF to high achievements. And he has made himself a heap of money while doing so.

Given that Heenan is a scheming, deceitful rascal, he has preferred wrestlers who opt for cheap shots and are willing to take shortcuts to success. Among his protégés have been Mr. Perfect, whom Heenan guided to the Intercontinental Championship; the brutal Haku and ruthless Barbarian; and the burly Hercules. And, although he says he no longer manages, when Ric Flair entered the WWF in 1991, Heenan quickly became his Financial Adviser.

The Brain prides himself on getting other people involved in his chicanery. "There are plenty of friends out there willing to help me if I ask them," says Heenan.

He's right. Back in 1990, for example, Heenan enlisted the help of the Million Dollar Man Ted DiBiase to regain the Intercontinental Title for Mr. Perfect. Mr. P had lost it a few months before to the Texas Tornado, and a rematch was quickly arranged. DiBiase bribed his way into being named guest ring announcer for the event. To make a long story short, after the referee was accidentally knocked out, DiBiase whacked the Tornado over the head with the title belt as he was pinning an unconscious Mr. Perfect for the victory. DiBiase then put a groggy Perfect atop the Tornado. The referee came to and declared Perfect the winner.

Heenan is proud of such trickery. "You ham-and-egger humanoids out there don't know what to make of me, do you?" smirks the Brain. "Well,

Above: The broadcast journalist.
Left: Heenan gets caught in the act.

don't even try. You can't fathom what's going on in my mind. I've got more tricks up my sleeve than the Bushwhackers have fleas. And now I'm going to be the world's best broadcast journalist."

Journalist? Maybe. Admittedly, Heenan is a commentator on *WWF Wrestling Challenge*, a co-host of USA's *Prime Time Wrestling* and a columnist for *WWF Magazine*. But the Brain's "journalism" consists of diatribes about people he doesn't like — people such as Hulk Hogan, Hacksaw Jim Duggan and everyone else in the WWF who is a straight-shooter. Heenan's journalism is like he is — yellow to the core. ∎

From:
Beverly Hills, California

Birthday:
November 3

Managerial style:
A cunning, crafty plotter adept at convincing other people to do his dirty work, too cowardly for much blatant interference, prefers subterfuge

Goal:
To win a Pulitzer Prize

Bobby "The Brain" Heenan

Jimmy "Mouth of the South" Hart

From:
Memphis, Tennessee

Birthday:
January 1

Managerial style:
Raucous, constant distraction of the referee

Goal:
Gold belts on the wall

Jimmy "Mouth of the South" Hart gives his Mountie instructions at ringside. The Mouth is one of the WWF's most successful managers.

For such a scrawny rabbit of a guy, Jimmy "Mouth of the South" Hart is very dangerous. Behind the shades that cover his eyes, beneath the whining and incessant jabbering that come from his mouth lurks a vicious streak a mile wide. Hart is a thief, a sneak and a backstabber. His forte is an uncanny ability to distract referees, accomplished by constant yammering — often enhanced by his megaphone — at ringside. He manages to interfere in matches and, more often than not, get

away with it. The Mouth also is a brilliant planner who likes to devise Byzantine plots to forward the ambitions of his wrestlers.

And wrestlers he has, aplenty. Throughout his career, Hart has always been able to maintain a large squad of awesome matmen, all of whom seem to complement one another. He has managed Intercontinental Champions and WWF Tag Team Champions. Recently in Hart's camp, for example, have been the Mountie, whose form of police brutality has made him feared throughout the WWF; the thuggish Nasty Boys, Knobbs and Sags; and the gargantuan Natural Disasters, Earthquake and Typhoon.

Hart, in fact, put the Natural Disasters together after convincing Typhoon, who was formerly known as Tugboat, to stop playing by the rules and join the Mouth's camp.

"I told that big man to get smart, baby," says Hart of his negotiations with Typhoon. "I made him realize he was wasting his time and that I'd get him to the top. He listened, and I signed him on."

In the Natural Disasters and Nasty Boys, Hart had two of the most dangerous tag teams ever to wrestle in the WWF. Most managers opt for only one team, not wanting competition within their own ranks. But Hart plays his teams like chess pieces. Seeking a WWF Tag Team Championship, at *WrestleMania VII* he set the Nasty Boys against the Hart Foundation, who held the belts. The Nasty Boys won, with the help of the Mouth's interference, and took the title home. However, at *SummerSlam* a few months later, the Nastys were beaten by the Legion of Doom. Tenaciously, Hart went after the title again,

this time not using the Natural Disasters. Instead he dumped them, took on IRS and the Million Dollar Man Ted DiBiase and led them to the title. ■

....

They call him the Music Man because of his background as a rock band star. The plots that Jimmy Hart composes leave his foes with a sour note.

66 **I work hard for my men, daddy. I've got their best interests at heart — or, should I say, at Hart.** 99

Paul Bearer

From:
Unknown

Birthday:
Unknown

Managerial style:
Unspoken support for the Undertaker, apparently with the aid of a funeral urn

Goal:
Hard to fathom

Paul Bearer is genuinely creepy. With his hunched shoulders and twisted face, he prowls at ringside like a ghoul, while between the ropes his Undertaker wreaks mayhem on opponents. Bearer carries a bronze urn clutched to his body. The urn goes almost everywhere he does, but it is especially important when the Undertaker is in the ring. It appears as if the Undertaker draws some strange form of power from the urn or whatever may be inside it. This force, weird as it sounds, enhances the Undertaker's strength, which even without help seems superhuman.

"In his own strange way," says WWF television commentator Gorilla Monsoon, "Paul Bearer is a very effective manager. I'll admit, though, that even I can't quite figure out his style. Still, who knows what goes on between Paul Bearer and the Undertaker away from the ring, out of sight? Actually, maybe we wouldn't want to find out."

Unlike most other managers, Paul Bearer seldom, if ever, physically interferes in a match. Nor does he go out of his way to distract the referee. However, his very presence is so unnerving that it impairs the Undertaker's foes on a psychological level. Who can concentrate on wrestling when a weirdo like Bearer is hovering nearby, watching like a vulture over a dying man?

Once the Undertaker wins a match, Bearer has other tasks. He unravels the body bag in which the Undertaker stuffs his beaten opponents. Then Bearer reads the fallen foe his last rites before the Undertaker carts him away.

Paul Bearer also hosts a television interview segment, *The Funeral Parlor*, on the *WWF Superstars of Wrestling*. Guests enter at their own peril. They never know what fate awaits them in the Parlor. Hulk Hogan, for instance, was ambushed and severely beaten by the Undertaker during a *Funeral Parlor* interview. Other guests — depending on the frame of Paul Bearer's strange mind — are welcomed by Bearer and visit *The Funeral Parlor* at no risk.

"Some people come to *The Funeral Parlor* in the right frame of mind," says Bearer in a voice that quavers like a screech owl's eerie call. "They are respectful of the dead and are in no danger. But others who lack that respect sometimes have their problems. Oh yes, when they enter the realm of Paul Bearer and the Undertaker, you see, they really do walk in the shadow of death." ∎

Left: Even Paul Bearer didn't like Jake the Snake's cobra. *Right:* Paul's funeral urn provides the Undertaker with a source of truly strange power.

He drives them, goads them and brutalizes them.

Clad in formal attire, scraping, bowing and forever smiling, Mr. Fuji seems to be the epitome of etiquette and courtesy. It is a sham. Mr. Fuji is one of the most unscrupulous and lethal individuals in the WWF, maybe anywhere. Fuji is innately cruel and truly enjoys seeing other people suffer. This applies not only to the opponents of his wrestlers, but to his own protégés as well.

Mr. Fuji is infamous for the way he treats his wrestlers. He puts them through grueling training designed not only to toughen their bodies but also to harden their minds. Fuji purposely commits training excesses that cause pain, feeling that these methods will make his men almost as cruel and ruthless as he is when they enter the squared circle.

"Suffering good for wrestlers," says Mr. Fuji. "It make them tough. Make them want to win in bad way. That why Mr. Fuji give his men pain. So they give pain to others."

It seems to work for the treacherous Mr. Fuji. Historically, his charges have been inordinately barbaric in the ring — and none more so that the Berzerker. This ferocious Northman from Iceland acts like a wild man, tearing into opponents like a wolf into raw meat. Typical of the wrestlers that Mr. Fuji has managed, the Berzerker is totally under his control, brainwashed if you will. Fuji claims that he controls the Berzerker with a form of telepathy called "mind-to-mind communication." Whether this is true or not no one can say, but Fuji does seem able to direct the Berzerker's fury without using a spoken word.

Fuji himself is a physically dangerous man. Other managers plan and plot. So does Fuji. Unlike most of the others, however, he poses the threat of physical harm to the opponent of whomever he has sent into the ring. Mr. Fuji's cane, for example, has been wielded by the manager with lethal effectiveness on numerous occasions. He uses it like a club, cracking it across head and shoulders. Or he employs it as a spear, jabbing it point-first into ribs. It also serves as a hook, slipped under the ropes to trip a victim.

"My cane," says Mr. Fuji, "is only tool. It is tool to teach discipline. Mr. Fuji think discipline very good for people, just like suffering. And Mr. Fuji very good at teaching people about discipline and suffering. Very good, indeed." ■

....

Don't let that smile fool you. Mr. Fuji is a cruel man, even to his own wrestlers.

From:
Osaka, Japan

Birthday:
May 4

Managerial style:
Physically and psychologically driving his wrestlers to the brink of their endurance

Goal:
To torture all opponents

Mr. Fuji

Harvey Wippleman

From:
He won't say

Birthday:
February 29

Managerial style:
A rah-rah boy

Goal:
To push people around

Harvey Wippleman is a typical milquetoast who wishes he were big, strong, handsome and charming. He isn't. He's a skinny little runt with a toady personality and the courage of an earthworm. Harvey likes to throw his weight — scant as it is — around. Since he can't manage to do that on his own — he wouldn't frighten a baby rabbit — he likes to associate with guys who are big and brawny, the tougher the better.

Thus, Harvey decided that becoming a manager in the WWF was the job for him. As a manager of one big brute or another, he could earn a living and vicariously be a tough guy. Although Harvey had little in the way of managerial skills, he did have something to offer. He could cater to ego, fawning over and cheering for whichever wrestler decided to engage him. He found one: a very big, tough guy, indeed — Sid Justice.

"Yeah," simpers Harvey, "Sid Justice can shove around anybody he wants. Sid Justice and I, we're a force to be reckoned with in the WWF. Nobody better get in our way. We're mean, man. We are real bad dudes. Anybody want to try us? We're ready to tangle."

Right, Harvey. Sid Justice is ready to battle anybody but Harvey scuttles for cover as soon as things get hot. Admittedly, he sometimes tries interference. But if somebody even scowls at him, he runs for cover. Deep down, apparently, Harvey knows that a wimp will always be a wimp. ∎

After Sid Justice demolishes an opponent, his manager, Dr. Harvey Wippleman, examines the beaten foe for signs of life.

From:
Baghdad, Iraq

Birthday:
March 3

Managerial style:
Dictatorial and militaristic

Goal:
Conquest

General Adnan

General Adnan's hero is Attila, the ancient leader of the terrible Huns. He waged war so ruthlessly that he was known as the "Scourge of God." Adnan has patterned his managerial strategy after the military tactics of Attila. Once an opponent is in the ring, even if the bell has not sounded, Adnan declares war.

Steeped in hatred for the United States, Adnan enjoyed targeting American wrestlers who pride themselves on serving their country. His greatest conquest was the subversion of Sgt. Slaughter, that superb patriot who had always put his country before all else. Subtly at first, Adnan ensnared Slaughter with catering to his love for the military. "Might," said Adnan, "makes right." Then Adnan began to play on Slaughter's sense of justice. "You've done so much for your country, Sergeant Slaughter," asked the crafty Adnan, "but what has your country done for you? Why aren't you the WWF Champion?" Finally, Slaughter was won over by Adnan's words, and the general held him psychological hostage.

Adnan, later aided by his ally Colonel Mustafa, launched Slaughter against WWF Champion Ultimate Warrior. In a controversial decision, Slaughter won the belt, only to lose it at *WrestleMania VII* to Hulk Hogan. With the title lost, Adnan turned viciously on Slaughter. It was the best thing that could have happened to the Sarge because he realized the error of his ways and returned to his country.

Adnan was left abandoned by the very man he had tried to subvert. Typical of Adnan, he beat a hasty retreat. He had no stomach for war without Slaughter taking the point. ∎

For all his bravado and medals, General Adnan was exposed as a coward who lets others do his fighting for him.

The Genius

From:
Downers Grove, Illinios

Birthday:
December 28

Managerial style:
Extremely cerebral

Goal:
To become even smarter

. . . .

With the Beverly Brothers at his side, the Genius spouts off with some of his horrendous poetry, liable to bore his foes to death.

The Genius, manager of the Beverly Brothers, proclaims himself to be the "world's smartest man." He is given to writing poetry, more often than not mocking the opponents of his Beverlys in verse. Smug beyond belief, the Genius fancies himself to be on an intellectual level far above that of ordinary people. "Who is an intellectual equal of mine?" he asks. "Maybe no one, except possibly Dr. Einstein."

The managerial genius of the Genius has yet to be proved. However, he has brought the Beverly Brothers, Beau and Blake, into top WWF competition and claims that he'll keep them up there. ■

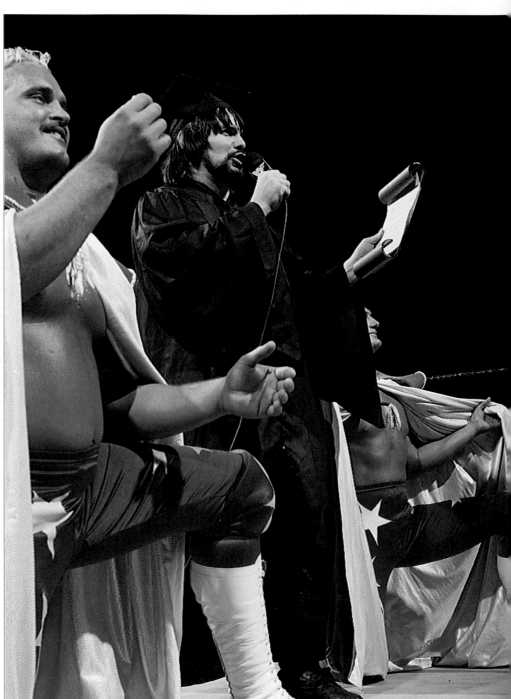

Sensational Sherri came into her own as a manager after the Mega-Powers were sundered and Macho Man Randy Savage became the Macho King. As the Sensational Queen, Sherri prodded the Macho King to commit dastardly deeds, all the while claiming her wicked advice was solely for his bene-

Since then, she has hooked up with Shawn Michaels. Spiteful and vindictive, she readily interferes in his matches, tripping his opponents and socking them with foreign objects such as her loaded purse. Sherri is as witchy as she is gorgeous. She claws and spits like a cat and howls like a she-wolf. Some of her detractors have

From:
New Orleans, Louisiana

Birthday:
February 8

Managerial style:
Witchy types of interference, perhaps as dangerous as Mr. Fuji

Goal:
To make herself the wealthiest manager in the WWF

Sensational Sherri

fit. In reality, she was out for herself, using Savage to get ahead. That fact was revealed when Savage lost his retirement match with the Ultimate Warrior at *WrestleMania*. Furious at the loss of her meal ticket, Sherri turned on Savage like a tigress.

She quickly found another wrestler. Sherri was hired by the Million Dollar Man Ted DiBiase to manage him.

called her "Scary Sherri." That's a good assessment of her. She is certainly one scary lady.

Her own words prove it. "I'll do anything I can to further the cause of my Shawn," she says. "If anybody thinks they can mess with him, they've also got to mess with me. And, boys, my nails are sharp enough to gouge steel." ∎

Sensational Sherri is one of the World Wrestling Federation's most active managers at ringside. She's down and dirty — and dangerous.

WRESTLEMANIA RULES

WrestleMania was the first of the WWF's events on pay-per-view cable television. Since the first *WrestleMania* in 1985, this extraordinary wrestling spectacular has become a worldwide tradition.

WrestleMania

In some ways, the inaugural *WrestleMania*, held March 31, 1985, at New York's Madison Square Garden, was the most special one. Never before had such a large audience witnessed a wrestling match as those present in the arena and those viewing the action on closed-circuit telecasts and the infant medium of pay-per-view television — a technology that the World Wrestling Federation would soon develop and claim as its very own.

The Rock 'n' Wrestling Connection was a central theme of the night, as WWF Women's Champion Leilani Kai, managed by perennial titlist the Fabulous Moolah, dropped her championship belt to Wendi Richter, managed by none other than rock star Cyndi Lauper — then at the peak of her singing career.

Boxing great Muhammad Ali was the special referee, and Liberace was the guest timekeeper.

Lauper was one of the most fervent Hulkamaniacs. Prior to the historic event, she went around the United States extolling the virtues of WWF Champion Hulk Hogan, who had won the World Wrestling Federation Championship Belt for the first time the year before. When Rowdy Roddy Piper — then known as "the man you love to hate" — condemned rock 'n' roll, Lauper vowed that her friend the Hulkster would gain revenge in the main event.

Hogan teamed with television and film star Mr. T — they had met when both were featured in the film *Rocky III* — in an unforgettable contest against Piper and Paul "Mr. Wonderful" Orndorff.

Seldom had a match been so wild. With the capacity crowd in a state of euphoria, T proved that he could mix it up with the big boys, as he surprised Piper with a fireman's carry and dumped him on the canvas. Soon Hogan was in, atomic-dropping Piper, then ganging up with the rugged actor to double-whip and clothesline the Rowdy Scot. It was only after Orndorff smashed the champion with a foreign object — and Piper bashed him with a chair outside the ring — that the unpopular pair gained an edge in the match.

Mr. T rushed to his teammate's aid, relying on street-fighting techniques he picked up on the rough streets of Chicago. The match continued at a furious pace until everyone was brawling in the squared circle. As Hogan struggled with the brawny Orndorff, Piper's "bodyguard" Cowboy Bob Orton jumped in and tried to slam his arm cast on the titlist's head. But Hogan moved, and the weapon crashed down on Mr. Wonderful, who looked less than fabulous as he fell to the canvas and was pinned by the Hulkster.

Hulkamania was already an established institution. From this moment on, *WrestleMania* would become a household word as well. ∎

A violent all-out brawl erupted at the first *WrestleMania* between Hulk Hogan and partner, Mr. T, and Paul "Mr. Wonderful" Orndorff and Rowdy Roddy Piper.

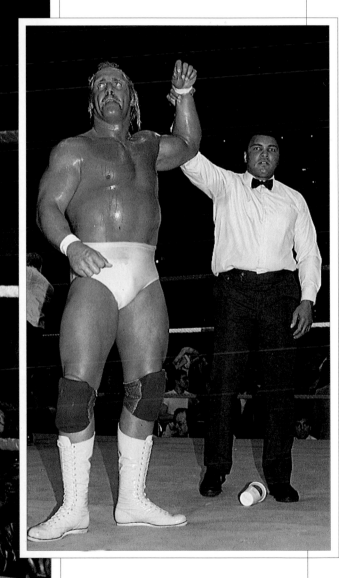

At the end of the match between Hogan and Mr. T and Piper and Orndorff, Muhammad Ali raises the Hulkster's hand in victory.

WrestleMania II

WrestleMania I was indeed a tough act to follow, but the WWF managed to top the historic spectacular the next year with an event held at three separate arenas and broadcast around the world via satellite. On April 7, 1986, at New York's Nassau Coliseum, Piper and Mr. T continued their battle from the previous year, engaging in a special boxing match. The same night, at the Los Angeles Sports Arena, Hulk Hogan defended his belt — in a steel cage — against monstrous King Kong Bundy. And, in perhaps the most curious contest on the card, six National Football League players competed with 14 WWF superstars in an over-the-top-rope battle royal at Chicago's Rosemont Horizon.

Comedienne Joan Rivers took on announcing duties at the Nassau Coliseum. Jazz legend Cab Calloway was a judge for the Piper-Mr. T pugilistic exchange. And blues-great Ray Charles started the evening off with his stirring rendition of *America the Beautiful*.

At the time, the 450-pound Bundy was one of the most dreaded men in the WWF and had recently injured Hogan with a series of avalanches — splashes against the corner of the ring. The Hulkster entered the steel cage with bruised ribs, but he came ready to fight.

It was a thunderous battle. The end came after Hogan had disabled Bundy with a legdrop. The Hulkster attempted to score the victory by climbing out of the cage. Bundy rose off the canvas and tried to pull the champion back down into the center of the ring. The Hulkster kicked his foe away, but Bundy's manager, Bobby "The Brain" Heenan, scaled the bars from the outside of the cage and attempted to block the champion's departure. Hogan knocked the adviser out of the way and continued his journey, scoring the win. Then, he pulled Heenan into the cage, punishing him with an atomic drop.

Both competitors came well-prepared for the Piper-Mr. T matchup: "Hot Rod" was seconded by former U.S. Olympic boxing coach Lou Duva, while T's adviser was ex-Heavyweight Boxing Champion Smokin' Joe Frazier. The problem was that Piper really didn't want to box — when he shoved the referee and bodyslammed his opponent, he was disqualified.

In the battle royal, the focus of media attention was 304-pound William "Refrigerator" Perry of the Chicago Bears, but his hopes were dashed when Big John Studd eliminated him. Andre the Giant — the king of the battle royals — eventually logged the victory, throwing out Jim "The Anvil" Neidhart and his partner, Bret "Hit Man" Hart, in the final moments. ■

. . . .

After a titanic steel cage match against King Kong Bundy, Hogan scored the win by ascending the bars and climbing out of the cage. Hogan, however, took a beating.

Once again, the stars turned out.

WrestleMania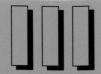

Undefeated throughout his career, Andre the Giant had been friends with Hulk Hogan for several years. Because of that, the massive Andre had never received a title match against his friend. When the seven-foot-five-inch Giant decided that he wanted to go one-on-one with the champion, many fans were curious — so many, in fact, that a record 93,173 spectators crammed into the Pontiac Silverdome in Pontiac, Michigan, to witness the dream match, while millions more watched on pay-per-view.

....

At *WrestleMania III*, Andre the Giant was cleanly defeated for the first time.

The main event was filled with drama from the opening seconds.

The champion and challenger stood nose-to-nose, trying to stare each other down, as the fans screamed loud enough to be heard in Andre's native France. Hogan said something that apparently infuriated his former buddy, inducing the Giant to shove him. The Hulkster responded with several punches of his own, then tried a bodyslam. But Andre's weight was too much for the champion. Andre fell on top of the Hulkster and nearly pinned him.

From that point on, any semblance of friendship that ever existed between the pair evaporated. They brawled in the ring and outside of it. Eventually, they returned to the mat where Hogan unleashed a bodyslam, followed by the patented legdrop. For the first time ever, Andre was cleanly defeated.

Another classic skirmish was fought between WWF Intercontinental Champion Macho Man Randy Savage and Ricky "The Dragon" Steamboat. The two were evenly matched in this thrilling contest, and each came inches away from victory on several occasions. But the end came when Macho Man climbed the turnbuckles holding the time-keeper's bell and attempted to aggravate a larynx injury inflicted on the Dragon months earlier. But

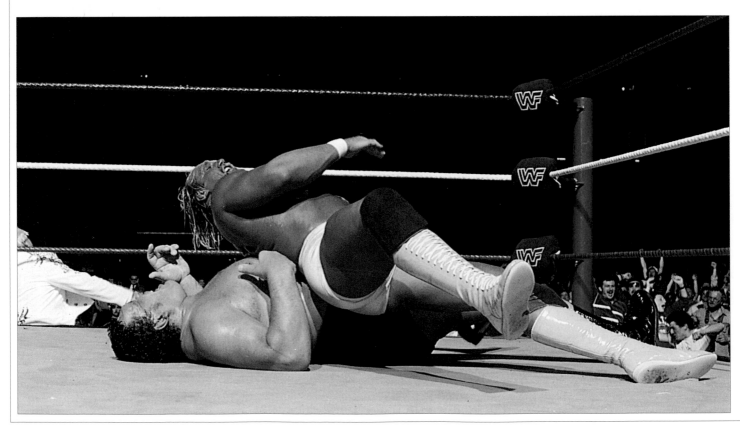

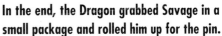

In the end, the Dragon grabbed Savage in a small package and rolled him up for the pin.

Steamboat's ally, George "The Animal" Steele, intervened, shoving Savage onto the canvas, where he was caught in a small package and pinned.

Hoping to pursue a career as a Hollywood actor, Rowdy Roddy Piper announced that his *WrestleMania III* match against the late Adrian Adonis would be his last. Having mended fences with the fans, Piper had the crowd behind him as he repeatedly embarrassed his obese adversary. The spectators were in an ecstatic frenzy as Piper had his way with his foe and Adonis' manager, Jimmy "Mouth of the South" Hart, who was hurled on top of his protégé when he tried to attack the Scotsman from the top rope. After Piper disposed of his opponent with a sleeperhold, Brutus "The Barber" Beefcake entered the ring, seeing his chance to avenge an earlier haircutting episode by giving Adorable Adrian an embarrassing clipping. ∎

The Dragon and Savage clash.

WrestleMania IV

What started as one of the most bizarre incidents in the history of the WWF ended on March 27, 1988, at Trump Plaza Hotel and Casino in Atlantic City, New Jersey — as Macho Man Randy Savage won a special tournament to become the WWF Champion.

For the first time ever, the WWF title had been declared vacant when Andre the Giant — with the help of a corrupt referee paid off by Million Dollar Man Ted DiBiase — literally stole the championship from Hulk Hogan and then surrendered it to DiBiase. WWF President Jack Tunney ruled the title vacant and ordered the *WrestleMania IV* tourney to determine a new kingpin.

A who's who of main-eventers entered for the chance to win the most cherished prize in wrestling. Among them were DiBiase, Hacksaw Jim Duggan, the Magnificent Muraco, Bam Bam Bigelow, Ricky "The Dragon" Steamboat, Greg "The Hammer" Valentine and Jake "The Snake" Roberts.

Andre and Hogan were the favorites, but their chances for victory were dashed when their tempers got the better of them. Their match ended when, in the heat of the furious action, each forgot about the rules and reached for a chair. While they dueled with the objects, the referee called for a double disqualification.

Still, both had interest in the final contest, pitting DiBiase — who earlier triumphed over Duggan and Muraco — against Macho Man — who had vanquished Butch Reed, Greg "The Hammer" Valentine and One Man Gang. While Savage and the Million Dollar Man fought between the ropes, Hogan and Andre were conspicuous at ringside.

With Andre's help, DiBiase gained an advantage over Savage. But when the Giant tried to drag a half-conscious Macho Man from the ring, the Hulkster intervened, blasting the mammoth Frenchman with a punch, then sitting down and demanding

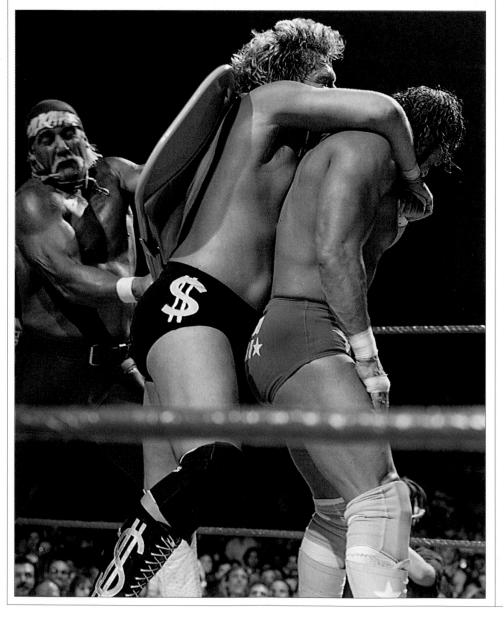

Hulk Hogan saves an exhausted Macho Man Randy Savage by whacking the Million Dollar Man Ted DiBiase with a chair.

DiBiase had received a bye because, due to the double disqualification of Hulk and Andre, there was no one to challenge him in the third round. The Million Dollar Man was fresher than Savage.

that the battle resume.

Still, Savage was weak, and DiBiase was able to capitalize on the situation. When the Macho Man missed a flying elbow, the Million Dollar Man nearly won it all with a sleeperhold. Savage reached for the ropes to save himself, but Andre pulled the strand away.

Now, Hogan came to the rescue. With the referee distracted, the Hulkster smashed DiBiase with a chair, allowing Savage to again mount the ropes, lower the flying elbow and gain the triumph and the coveted championship.

Savage celebrated his win in the center of the ring, surrounded by his two closest allies: his manager Elizabeth and the Hulkster. The three professed loyalty to one another and, to the outsider's eye, appeared aligned for life. But one short year later a disagreement in the Macho Man's camp would ignite the main event at *WrestleMania V*. ∎

A gracious Hulkster congratulates Macho Man Randy Savage after Savage triumphed in the *WrestleMania IV* tourney.

WrestleMania V

Once again, wrestling's grandest event returned to Trump Plaza Hotel & Casino in Atlantic City, New Jersey. But the allegiances were far different this year. Hulk Hogan and Macho Man Randy Savage — who formed the Mega-Powers after the victory at *WrestleMania IV* — were enemies in the main event on April 2, 1989, at *WrestleMania V*.

No one had to do much guessing to figure out the cause. Savage's manager, Elizabeth, had done her best to support both men as they battled in tag team matches as the Mega-Powers. Instead, her presence — and the Macho Man's jealousy — tore the team apart.

Weeks earlier the Mega-Powers were pitted against the Twin Towers, Big Boss Man and the enormous Akeem, in a match seen on the NBC television network. When Savage was hurled from the ring in the course of the contest, he landed on Elizabeth at ringside, knocking her out. Seeing the beautiful manager injured, Hogan carried her to the dressing room, leaving his partner alone with their opponents.

Although the Hulkster would later return and Macho Man would score the victory, the champion accused his partner of abandoning him and "having lust for Elizabeth." As they argued in the dressing room, Savage attacked the Hulkster and Elizabeth. In response, Hogan asked for a title shot against his former partner at *WrestleMania V*.

During the main event, Elizabeth was in the Hulkster's corner, mainly because she felt she had no other choice. Believing that Macho Man was at fault in the Mega-Powers' break-up, she agreed to side with the Hulkster.

During his earlier dressing room attack, Savage had grabbed her arm and slung her across the room when she tried to protect Hogan.

Savage used every underhanded tactic he knew to try to defeat Hogan this night, then climbed the ropes and delivered the lethal flying elbow. But the wishes of the Hulka-maniacs proved to be more potent. His legions cheering him on, Hogan rose from the brink of defeat, delivering an Irish whip, a big boot and a legdrop before reclaiming his belt.

Earlier in the evening, WWF Intercontinental Champion Ultimate Warrior was defeated by Ravishing Rick Rude. After expelling Rude from the ring, Warrior suplexed his foe — from the apron — back between the ropes. But, from ringside, Rude's manager, Bobby "The Brain" Heenan, hooked Warrior's leg. Rude fell on top of his foe — and Heenan continued to grasp the limb while the referee counted to three. As Rude strapped the Intercontinental Belt around his waist, Warrior felt nothing but sheer agony, never imagining that at the next *WrestleMania* he would enjoy the most glorious moment of his career. ■

Things were different at *WrestleMania V*, when Hulk and Savage were foes. After a bruising battle, the Hulkster whipped the Macho Man and regained the title.

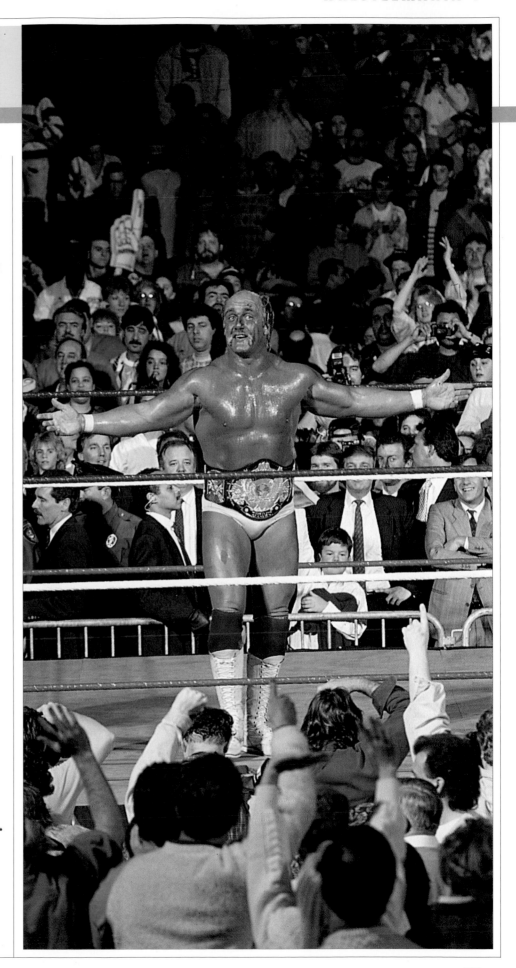

WrestleMania VI

It was a proud day for Canada when *WrestleMania VI* was held on April 1, 1990, in front of 67,678 fans at Toronto's Sky-Dome. Singer Robert Goulet got the crowd in a patriotic mood when he began the festivities with his rendition of *O Canada*. Actress Mary Tyler Moore sat in the front row and seemed a bit shocked when Jake "The Snake" Roberts — then among the best-liked men in the ring — snatched a $100 bill from Million Dollar Man Ted DiBiase and handed it to her.

However, the night had the Ultimate Warrior's signature written all over it. He had regained the Intercontinental Belt and now challenged Hogan for his title. Although both men came at each other with everything they had, they remained friends throughout the battle and even embraced when it was all over.

As wrestling styles go, this was not a technical matchup, but one between two gladiators exploding with atomic force. At one point, the referee could not evade the fury of the ring and ended up on the mat, unconscious. Hogan finally sidestepped the Warrior, drove his head into the mat and went for the cover. But the referee was still out.

Eventually, the referee came to, and Warrior seemed on a roll. He clotheslined the Hulkster, slammed him after a gorilla press and gained a two-count following a big splash.

But Hogan was not finished yet. He sprang off the canvas and weath-ered his foe's punches. Then he whipped Warrior off the ropes and delivered a boot to the chin. With Warrior down, the Hulkster started to execute his reliable finisher, the leg-drop. But then something happened: Warrior moved out of the way. Hogan crashed to the mat, writhing in pain. The Warrior gave his opponent no time to recuperate. He big-splashed Hogan, covered him and became the first wrestler to earn a clean pinfall over the Hulkster.

Hogan was gracious in defeat and remained a loyal ally of the Warrior after the match, teaming with him regularly.

Earlier, an old Hogan nemesis had a change of heart. After Andre the Giant and Haku lost the WWF Tag Team Title to Demolition, Haku and manager Bobby Heenan turned on Andre. Realizing their treachery, Andre dumped them from the ring and vowed to walk on the right side of the street again. ■

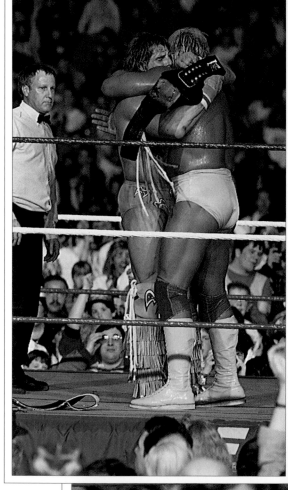

When the Hulkster and the Ultimate Warrior went title for title at *WrestleMania VI*, each man was pushed far beyond his physical and emotional limits. The Warrior emerged the victor.

Normally, these competitors would have halted the war and tended to the official. But this was different — winning meant everything.

WrestleMania VII

To many observers, *Wrestle-Mania VI* seemed the changing of the guard, with Hulk Hogan passing the gauntlet to the Ultimate Warrior. But when peculiar circumstances changed the face of the WWF title picture, Hogan stepped in to save the day. By March 24, 1991, the date of *WrestleMania VII*, Sgt. Slaughter — then a supporter of dictatorship and tyranny — was the WWF Champion, having acquired the belt at the previous *Royal Rumble* with the help of Randy Savage's interference. The Hulkster arrived at the Los Angeles Sports Arena determined to win back the belt.

Slaughter was at his best outside the ring, where his manager, General Adnan, became involved in the fray and was battered by Hogan. But while the Hulkster was busy with the manager, Slaughter seized the lead — with the help of a chair. Although Hogan rallied for a while, the Sarge again lured his foe to the ringside area. Slaughter slammed Hogan's head into a ring post and choked him with a television cable.

Returning to the mat, the Sarge trapped Hogan in a Boston crab. The Hulkster fought free, but Slaughter bloodied his opponent with a chair to the cranium and nearly scored a victory with a camel clutch.

But overconfidence would prove to be Slaughter's undoing.

Sgt. Slaughter tries to strangle a downed Hulkster at *WrestleMania VII*. Slaughter's dirty tricks did him no good. Hogan took the title away from him.

Believing that Hogan was too weak to defend himself, the Sarge attempted to humiliate him by covering his body with the Iraqi flag. Outraged, the Hulkster reached down and found new strength. He rose to his feet and ripped up the enemy banner, then unloaded on Slaughter and finished him with a legdrop. Months later, the Sarge admitted that Hogan was the better man that night and renounced his anti-American views.

Hogan might have captured the belt, but Randy Savage claims he won the real prize at *WrestleMania VII*. After being vanquished in a "loser must retire" match to the Ultimate Warrior, a barely conscious Savage was attacked by his manager, Sensational Sherri, who slammed his head against the mat. Unable to witness the disgraceful spectacle, Elizabeth, who was in the audience, raced down the aisle, pounced on Sherri and — relying more on emotion than strength — hurled Sherri to the ringside floor. When Savage came to and realized what had transpired, he embraced Elizabeth and asked her to forgive him for forsaking her. Within a matter of months the two were married, and the "retirement" stipulation of the match was overturned. ■

GET TO GRIPS WITH WWF

In addition to *WrestleMania,* the WWF presents several other annual spectaculars over pay-per-view cable television. Each has its unique blend of action and drama. And like *WrestleMania,* each has created major turning points in WWF history.

THE ROYAL RUMBLE

of which was to be declared undisputed WWF Champion. Flair, exhibiting incredible persistence and endurance, drew No. 3 and thus entered the ring after only two minutes had passed. Using all of his cunning, gained from years of ring experience, Flair pulled out all the stops. He took cheap shots when he

Starting in January 1988, the WWF's *Royal Rumble* is a unique event in wrestling. Its highlight is a 30-man battle royal. Wrestlers are eliminated by being ousted from the ring over the top rope. The last man in the ring is the winner. Given that it is every man for himself, there are no friends or allies in the *Royal Rumble*'s battle royal. Even tag team partners have gone at one another. What makes this battle royal different, however, is that wrestlers enter the ring by luck of the draw. They draw numbers by chance. Nos. 1 and 2 enter the ring first. Every two minutes after that, another wrestler enters, until the man who drew No. 30 is the last man to join the fray. This means that wrestlers who draw high numbers will be fresher than those who entered earlier.

The winner of the first *Royal Rumble* battle royal, on cable television but not yet on pay-per-view, was Hacksaw Jim Duggan, who entered 23rd. Big John Studd, who won the second, entered 27th. Hulk Hogan, winner of the next, entered 25th. Hulk won the following battle royal, too, after being drawn to enter midway through the contest.

Given what had happened before, Ric Flair astounded watchers at the January 1992 battle royal, the winner

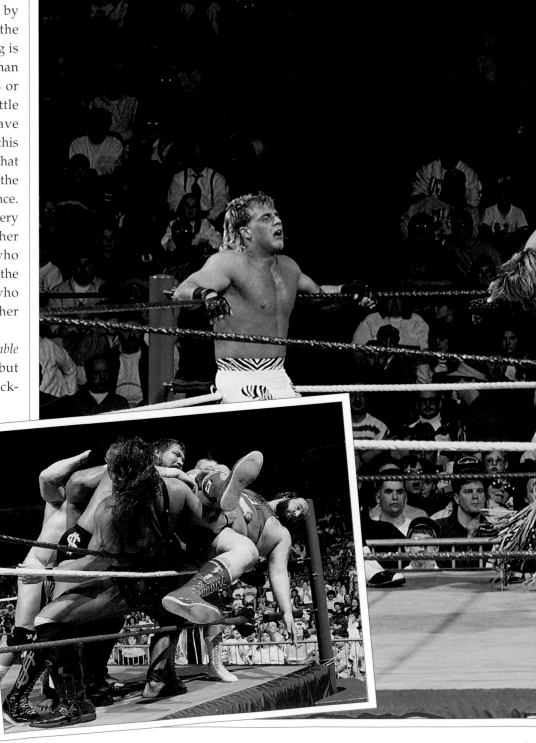

There are no friends at the *Royal Rumble*, where it's every man for himself in a 30-man battle royal. Each goes all out to be the last in the ring and, thus, the victor.

had the opportunity and rested when the chance presented itself. He also put on an astonishing display of wrestling talent and withstood a tremendous pounding, proving himself an athlete par excellence.

In the end, three men were in the ring — Flair, Hogan and Sid Justice. The latter two men had entered very late in the contest. Justice, in fact, was next to last. As Hogan tussled with Flair, Justice struck from behind and ousted the Hulkster. Flair then went for Justice. Meanwhile, the Hulkster reached up from the arena floor, grabbed Sid's arm and, with a mighty heave, yanked him from the ring. Standing in center ring, under the lights, only Ric Flair remained to claim the precious title. Possibly Flair had been lucky. At the same time, he had accomplished what no man had ever done: He had entered after only two minutes and remained to the end. Perhaps it was fitting that in this way Ric Flair won the title he so much desired. ■

AT THE 1991 ROYAL RUMBLE, SGT. SLAUGHTER TOOK THE WWF TITLE FROM THE ULTIMATE WARRIOR UNDER CONTROVERSIAL CIRCUMSTANCES.

SUMMERSLAM

The first *SummerSlam*, in 1988, was highlighted by the emergence of a new Intercontinental Champion, the Ultimate Warrior. His appearance on the card at New York City's Madison Square Garden was a surprise. The Honky Tonk Man, who held the championship belt, was to wrestle Brutus "The Barber" Beefcake. However, at the last minute, Brutus could not participate due to complications from an injury received in a previous match. The Warrior was put in as a substitute, something Honky didn't know until the challenger roared down the aisle to the ring.

The lovely Elizabeth came to the aid of the Mega-Powers at the first *SummerSlam*.

HONKY TONK NEVER KNEW WHAT HIT HIM.

The Ultimate Warrior celebrates after winning the belt from Honky Tonk.

The Warrior slid under the ropes and, as the bell sounded, tore into Honky. Battered and blasted, Honky Tonk was downed by a clothesline and pinned in a flash. It took only moments, but the title changed hands.

The feature match was also a stunner, but for different reasons. Mega-Powers Hulk Hogan and WWF Champion Macho Man Randy Savage were pitted against the Million Dollar Man Ted DiBiase and Andre the Giant. As the battle raged, Andre tried to illegally help DiBiase against Hogan. The Hulkster did something never before accomplished. He floored Andre with a single thunderous punch. With Andre down, Savage tried to bomb the Giant from the top rope, only to be met by a foot and kicked from the ring. Hulk, meanwhile, put a sleeper on DiBiase. Andre broke it up by headbutting the Hulkster, who also landed on the floor.

DESPITE THEIR GREAT VICTORY AT *SUMMERSLAM 1988*, THE MEGA-POWERS WOULD EVENTUALLY SELF-DESTRUCT. MACHO MAN BECAME JEALOUS OF WHAT HE THOUGHT WAS A GROWING LOVE RELATIONSHIP BETWEEN HULK AND ELIZABETH, WHO REALLY WERE ONLY FAST FRIENDS. AFTERWARD, HOGAN AND SAVAGE WOULD DO FIERCE BATTLE AT *WRESTLEMANIA V*. IN THAT MATCH, THE HULKSTER STRIPPED SAVAGE OF THE TITLE.

Things looked bleak for the Powers. Then Elizabeth acted. She jumped to the ring apron and whipped off her yellow skirt, revealing her shapely legs, shocking Andre and DiBiase. As they stood frozen, Savage mounted the ropes and crashed into Andre, flooring him. Hogan then slammed DiBiase, who suffered an elbow off the top buckle by Savage. Hogan covered the Million Dollar Man, and three seconds later the match belonged to the Mega-Powers. ∎

....

Hulk Hogan plants a boot in the midriff of the Million Dollar Man.

IN ANOTHER TURNABOUT, THE ULTIMATE WARRIOR, WHO HAD LOST HIS TITLE TO RAVISHING RICK RUDE, GOT IT BACK. THE WARRIOR ROCKED RUDE WITH A PRESS SLAM, THEN SPLASHED AND PINNED HIM.

Much had changed by *SummerSlam 1989* at the Meadowlands Arena in East Rutherford, New Jersey. The Mega-Powers had split apart.

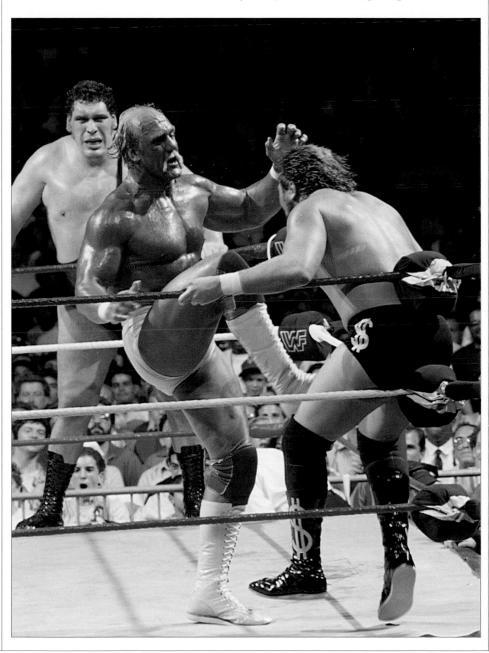

Hogan teamed with Brutus the Barber to battle Savage and Zeus, the Hulkster's nemesis in the film *No Holds Barred*. In the latter team's corner was Sensational Sherri, Savage's manager. Elizabeth was with Hogan and Beefcake.

Zeus seemed impervious to pain, hardly budging while the Hulkster unloaded blow after blow. It seemed as if nothing could keep Zeus from victory, until Hogan finally exploded and knocked him to one knee. Alarmed, Sherri, with her infamous loaded purse, tried to interfere. Then things happened rapid-fire. Elizabeth flipped her over the ropes to the mat. Savage grabbed the purse and tried to hammer Hogan with it from the top. Beefcake knocked him to the arena floor. The Hulkster picked up the purse and bashed Zeus with it, then covered him for the three-count. Bingo, it was over.

By *SummerSlam 1990*, held at the Spectrum in Philadelphia, Pennsylvania, the Warrior was WWF Champion. Again he met Ravishing Rick Rude, this time in a steel cage. After a bruising contest, the Warrior overwhelmed Rude with clotheslines and then gorilla-pressed and dropped him to the mat. Up and out of the cage went the Warrior, his title intact.

Two other titles changed hands. The young Texas Tornado surprised Mr. Perfect and took the Intercontinental Belt, while the Hart Foundation, consisting of Jim "The Anvil" Neidhart and Bret "Hit Man" Hart, grabbed the WWF Tag Team Belts from Smash and Crush of Demolition.

SummerSlam returned to Madison Square Garden in 1991. In a Match Made in Hell, WWF Champion Hulk

Hogan and the Ultimate Warrior took on the ruthless trio of Sgt. Slaughter, General Adnan and Colonel Mustafa. The match was extraordinary in that all but Adnan had at one time or another been a WWF Champion. Slaughter and his cohorts pulled out all the stops, using chokes, double-teams and even triple-teams against the Hulkster and his partner. It was a bruising battle, the tide of which changed several times. In the end, Hogan faced Slaughter and, afire with *Hulkamania*, defeated him.

Slaughter lost the match, but in defeat he started on the road to regaining his honor and country. Infuriated by the loss, Adnan and

....

In a Match Made in Heaven, Macho Man Randy Savage and the lovely Elizabeth were married at *SummerSlam '91*. The radiant couple said the words in center ring.

Mustafa turned their backs on Slaughter, finally showing him that there is no honor among thieves.

Again titles changed hands, with Bret "Hit Man" Hart beating Mr. Perfect for the Intercontinental Belt and the Legion of Doom, Hawk and Animal, getting the WWF Tag Team Championship from the Nasty Boys, Knobbs and Sags. The tag team match was unusual in that the WWF sanctioned it as a no-disqualification, no-count-out contest. That meant there would be no decision without a clear-cut winner. It also meant no rules. This situation was just fine for the Nasty Boys, who think rules are for fools. Unfortunately for them, unrestrained brawling is the forte of Hawk and Animal, who were brought up on the mean streets of Chicago. The Legion of Doom got really nasty with the Nastys. ■

A Match Made in Hell — Hulk Hogan and the Ultimate Warrior took on the evil trio.

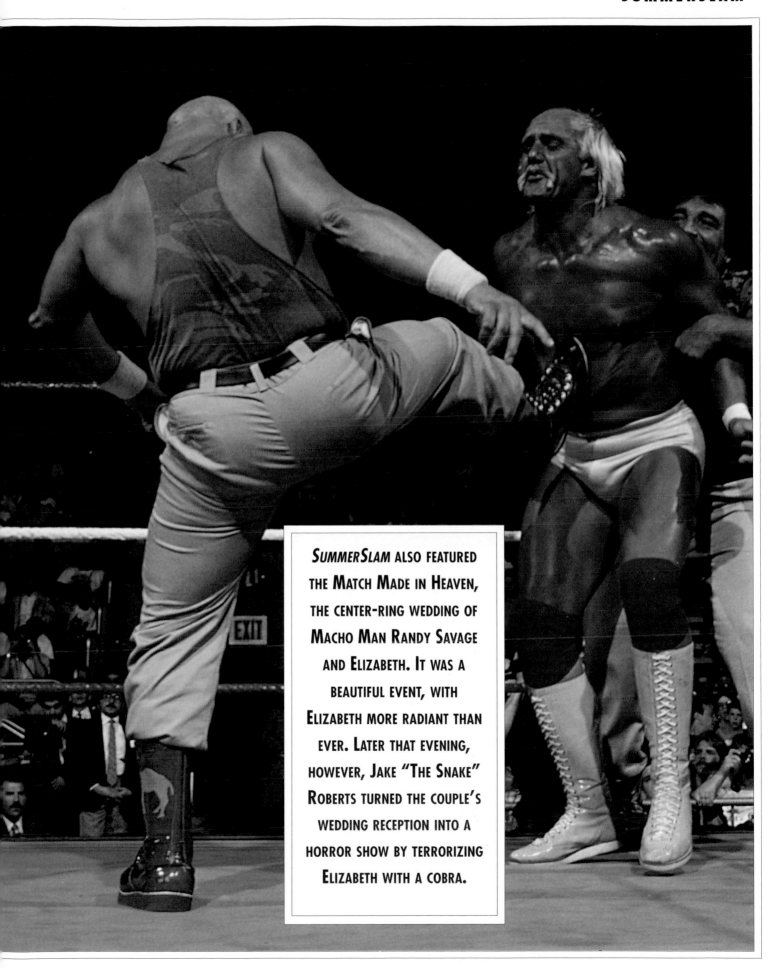

SummerSlam ALSO FEATURED THE MATCH MADE IN HEAVEN, THE CENTER-RING WEDDING OF MACHO MAN RANDY SAVAGE AND ELIZABETH. IT WAS A BEAUTIFUL EVENT, WITH ELIZABETH MORE RADIANT THAN EVER. LATER THAT EVENING, HOWEVER, JAKE "THE SNAKE" ROBERTS TURNED THE COUPLE'S WEDDING RECEPTION INTO A HORROR SHOW BY TERRORIZING ELIZABETH WITH A COBRA.

SURVIVOR SERIES

The *WWF Survivor Series*, held annually at U.S. Thanksgiving time, features matches between teams and sometimes individual matches as well. The rules state that competitors can tag in and out until they are eliminated. This continues until all members of one of the two competing teams have been eliminated. The system allows for interesting combinations. The last survivor of one team, for instance, could end up facing as many as four members of the other team.

The highlight of the first *Survivor Series*, in 1987 from the Richfield Coliseum near Cleveland, Ohio, was a battle between a team captained by Hulk Hogan and a team headed by Andre the Giant. Hogan, however, was eliminated by a count-out when he battled and bodyslammed the massive King Kong Bundy and One Man Gang on the arena floor. This left the last survivor of Hogan's team, Bam Bam Bigelow, to handle Andre, Bundy and the Gang. They squashed him.

The next *Survivor Series* also occurred at Richfield. Mega-Powers Hulk Hogan and Macho Man Randy Savage were still together, and they were the last survivors of their team. Outnumbered, they fought on against their opponents, Akeem, the Big Boss Man, the Million Dollar Man Ted DiBiase and Haku, who viciously attacked the pair, but in the end the Mega-Powers turned the tables. One by one their foes left the match until Hulk Hogan pinned Haku and scored the victory.

The 1989 *Survivor Series* exploded from the Rosemont Horizon in Rosemont, Illinois. Hulk Hogan and the Million Dollar Man, opposing cap-

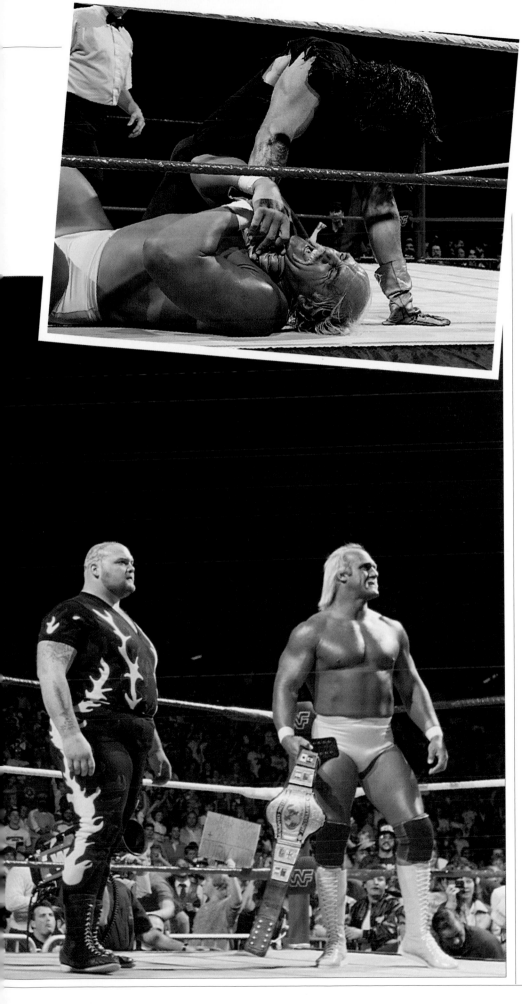

tains, ended up as the last survivors of their teams. The Million Dollar Man came out on the short end, pinned by the Hulkster. Mr. Perfect took honors for his squad by perfect-plexing and pinning Superfly Jimmy Snuka.

In 1990, the *Survivor Series* originated from the Hartford, Connecticut Civic Center. The event was highlighted by a match pitting the survivors of the four preceding team matches. It left Hulk Hogan, the Ultimate Warrior and Tito Santana against the Million Dollar Man Ted DiBiase and the entire team of the Model Rick Martel — the Warlord, and Power and Glory. Santana was eliminated early. But in the end, despite the odds, the Hulkster and Warrior survived after the Warrior pinned Hercules of Power and Glory.

The 1991 *Survivor Series* from the Joe Louis Arena in Detroit, Michigan, was an extraordinary event. The most important title in the World Wrestling Federation changed hands when Hulk Hogan lost the WWF Championship to the Undertaker.

In this *Series*, Ric Flair demonstrated his incredible cunning. He was teamed with the Million Dollar Man, the Mountie and Warlord against Rowdy Roddy Piper, Bret "Hit Man" Hart, Virgil and the British Bulldog. A brawl erupted outside the ring. Fists flew. It was chaos. Flair crept back into the ring. While the referee counted everyone else out, Flair stood between the ropes, a smug look on his face. He was the survivor. ■

Left: A scene from the first *Survivor Series.* *Above:* In a special WWF title match at the 1991 *Survivor Series,* the Undertaker beat Hulk Hogan and emerged with the belt.

THE WWF GOES GLOBAL

Although the roots of the World Wrestling Federation are in North America, fans of such superstar athletes as Hulk Hogan, Bret "Hit Man" Hart and Macho Man Randy Savage come from all over the globe.

In London neighborhoods like Wandsworth and Brixton, the Donnybrook section of Dublin and homes along the Clydeside Expressway in Glasgow, a generation of little Hulksters were training, saying their prayers and eating their vitamins just like their American soulmates.

· ·

They love the WWF in the UK.

The wrestling explosion in the United Kingdom is a phenomenon that has been compared with the British music invasion in the United States in the mid-1960s. Although there had previously been several tours of Europe, the WWF Rampage through England, Scotland and Ireland in the spring of 1991 is credited with altering the entertainment tastes in those countries forever.

While some WWF standouts — like the Big Boss Man, Legion of Doom and Nasty Boys — were busy settling unfinished business at American venues during the tour, UK fans were treated to matches involving Hulk Hogan, Jake "The Snake" Roberts, Rowdy Roddy

Piper, the Ultimate Warrior, Hacksaw Jim Duggan, the Undertaker, Earthquake, Mr. Perfect and Million Dollar Man Ted DiBiase, among others. Of course, the crowd choice at virtually every arena was the British Bulldog, who grew up near Manchester, England, and fought some of the greatest matches of his wrestling career on the tour to the delight of his ardent supporters.

"I can't describe the feeling I have, wrestling in front of all these beautiful people," the rugged Bulldog said after appearing — in front of an audience that included his mother and about one dozen other family members — at the Manchester G-Mex. "I think every British boy with wrestling ability dreams of being in

the World Wrestling Federation someday. To actually make it — and then come back and give your all in front of your hometown crowd — is indescribable."

On the other side of the ropes, Harvey Goldsmith, whose Allied Entertainment promoted the tour — along with MCP Promotions in Birmingham and Manchester — said he'd never seen fans so enthusiastic about an event. And that's from a man who's organized shows featuring Eric Clapton, the Rolling Stones and Madonna!

The "Tour de Force" — as the British press termed the trek — was sold out in six of the eight cities within hours after tickets went on sale. Tickets to the 11,000-seat Wem-

bley Arena in London were snapped up in less than an hour.

Merchandising records were set at every building: the Wembley and Docklands arenas in London, G-Mex, Brighton Centre, The Point in Dublin, Belfast Kings Hall, Glasgow SECC and the NEC Arena in Birmingham. WWF hats, T-shirts and posters outsold similar items available during a recent New Kids on the Block tour, and subscriptions for *WWF Magazine* — the largest imported publication in British history — skyrocketed.

The British Bulldog waves the Union Jack after winning a match during a tour of the UK. He loves wrestling live before fans in his homeland.

 I don't think I've ever been so up for a match in my entire life.
BRITISH BULLDOG

Then a cap — decorated with a shamrock and the word "Ireland" — sailed over the ropes, and the Rowdy Scot put it on his head.

As prohibitions eased in former Eastern bloc countries, wrestling fans there gained access to copies of *WWF Magazine* and videotapes of events like *WrestleMania* and *Summer-Slam*. Once the European tour was announced, devotees from what was formerly East Germany, as well as Hungary and Poland, took advan-

The Million Dollar Man Ted DiBiase and Sensational Sherri, then his manager, take a stroll around London during a WWF tour there.

tage of relaxed travel restrictions, purchased tickets and enjoyed their new freedom at the WWF events.

Certainly, there were classic moments in the ring: Hulk Hogan defeating Sgt. Slaughter at Wembley for the pride of all nations allied in the Persian Gulf War, the Bulldog's

thrilling victory over the Warlord at Docklands, Mr. Perfect's Intercontinental Championship Title battle against former champion El Matador Tito Santana in Brighton. But the high points of the tour usually transcended the action in the ring, as the WWF superstars and UK fans got to know each other.

Not every relationship was a positive one. DiBiase and his manager, Sensational Sherri, were followed by a group of children and roundly booed while walking down O'Connell Street in Dublin. The duo's reaction: waving a wad of Irish pounds at the critics while promising to dunk them in the Liffey River.

But most of the interaction was upbeat, such as Duggan's visit to the Brent Cross Mall in London, where he was mobbed by 3,000 followers, who trailed him from shop to shop, shouting "Hoooo!" in distinctly British accents.

When the Bulldog decided to pay homage to his queen by joining the crowd at Buckingham Palace for the changing of the guard, all attention shifted from the royal homestead to the Bulldog. In Birmingham, he was greeted by none other than rock idol Robert Plant of Led Zeppelin, who — after performing throughout his career in front of untold millions — had the chance to sit at ringside and enjoy the feeling of just being a fan.

While the Bulldog was the sentimental favorite at most venues, the fans also went wild over Scotsman Roddy Piper. Hot Rod, who was born in Glasgow but raised in Canada, viewed this trip as a special homecoming, and so did his supporters. In Dublin, he fought valiantly against DiBiase, eventually copping the win. No one anticipated what would occur next. In a spontaneous burst of enthusiasm for their fellow Celt, the "Dubs" — as residents of the Emerald Isle's capital city are called — broke into a moving Irish sports song. The "tri-color" — the nation's green, white and orange flag — was tossed into the ring and Piper picked it up and waved it proudly. With the serenade for the mat idol growing louder and louder, Piper soaked in the unique warmth that can only be found in the "Land of Saints and Scholars."

"Hot Rod'll have to check out this place again real soon," Piper later said in the dressing room. "You betcha."

A few short months later he was back, along with a host of other WWF superstars in a fall tour expanded to include Spain, France and Belgium.

In Barcelona, the WWF card prefaced the 1992 Olympics with a match at a stadium built specifically for the international sports competition. Spain's Tele Cinco television station provided live coverage, and fans quickly took to El Matador, who showed his appreciation of Spanish culture by discussing his bullfighting skills — acquired during an emotional trip to his native Mexico — with the local media.

In Paris, the show was covered live on Canal Plus. Surprisingly, the French could not restrain themselves from rising to their feet and chanting, "U-S-A! U-S-A!" in encouragement of Hacksaw Jim Duggan.

The natives were less receptive to Nasty Boys Knobbs and Sags.

When the Nastys got lost downtown, the locals pretended to possess no knowledge of English.

The tri-color was tossed into the ring to the popular Scotsman.

Rowdy Roddy Piper carries the Irish flag and receives an ovation from his fellow Celts in Dublin, Ireland.

History repeated itself; within 56 minutes after the spectacular was announced, every ticket for the London show was sold out. Again, much of the appeal was seeing such British Isles-born heroes as the British Bulldog and Rowdy Roddy Piper triumph. But a great deal of the excitement also simply came from sitting at ringside as such WWF superstars as the Legion of Doom, Undertaker, Nasty Boys, Mountie, Bret "Hit Man" Hart, Hacksaw Jim Duggan and Hercules strained their muscles and drowned in the perspiration of mat combat.

Left: Jimmy "Mouth of the South" Hart poses before a Beatles photo. *Below:* Hail, Bulldog! Young British fans back him each time he wrestles in the UK.

At the Royal Albert Hall, some attendees dressed in black tie, as if they were attending an opera, created a rousing chorus of cheers as the British Bulldog emerged victorious in a battle royal.

The Mountie momentarily stopped traffic while standing in the middle of Trafalgar Square, commanding all cars — and even double-decker buses — to halt. When he announced that he was an "international law officer" to guards at Buckingham Palace, their response was — not surprisingly — indifference.

The Mountie's manager, Jimmy "Mouth of the South" Hart invited himself to the original Hard Rock Café in London and was a bit surprised to find no mention of the Gentrys — his Memphis-based band from his teenage years, known for their hit *Keep on Dancin'* — or any of his protégés on the club's storied walls.

But while Hart and the Mountie were complaining about the "disrespect" shown them by the European fans, other WWF superstars were touched by the loyal followers who waited long hours outside the arenas and hotels to remind the athletes to come back soon. The wrestlers did not have to be prompted to return soon — the European fans, particularly those in Britain, are among the most appreciative in the world — but first there were battles to fight in other places. Virtually every night the titans of the WWF thrill spectators in the United States and Canada, but the mat wars have been waged in many other locations: the Middle East, Australia, Guam and Japan. ■

More-proper spectators admitted to being somewhat aghast at the sight of several fans attired not in formal wear but in the macabre funeral clothes of the dreaded Undertaker.

The Mountie tried to throw his weight around in London. He was lucky he didn't end up in the Tower.

Japan holds particular allure for the WWF competitors, largely because of the traditions associated with wrestling in the "Land of the Rising Sun." In the days after World War II, when the United States was helping the Japanese rebuild their society, the people of Japan gained a taste for two American passions: baseball and wrestling. The "sport of kings" — as the Japanese sometimes call it — has drawn capacity crowds since the 1950s, when men like future WWF manager Classy Freddy Blassie would travel across the Pacific to wrestle stars like the legendary Rikodozan. Current WWF announcer Gorilla Monsoon held several Japanese titles in the 1960s, when he tipped the scales at 401 pounds. In the 1970s Andre the Giant astounded the throngs in Tokyo and Yokohama with his incredible size, enormous strength and enviable wrestling ability. Just prior to winning his first WWF Championship, Hulk Hogan was heralded as Japan's most popular foreign star. Days after winning the belt, he returned to Tokyo, where

Inset: Million Dollar Man Ted DiBiase finds that his welcome to Japan is a rugged one.

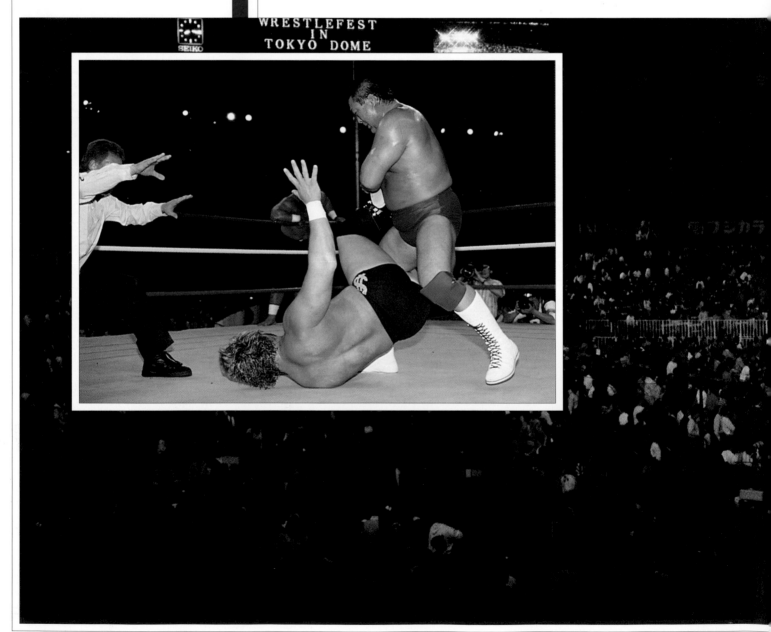

gleeful Hulkamaniacs greeted him at the airport with shouts of "Ichiban" — or "Number One."

The Hulkster was part of the contingent of WWF gladiators who delighted the city of Tokyo during the classic Nichi-Bei (Japanese-American) Wrestling Summit at the 63,000-seat Tokyo Dome — known as the "Big Egg." Limited Golden Ringside seats were available for 40,000 yen, as Hogan — along with other foreign favorites in Japan like Andre the Giant and Million Dollar Man Ted DiBiase — locked up with such prominent natives as Jumbo Tsuruta, Yoshi Yatsu, Masa Chono and Masa Saito. In a historic contest, Andre the Giant teamed with his longtime rival, Giant Baba — at one time, the tallest man in Japanese wrestling — to defeat Demolition.

Numerous WWF stars have returned to Japan after achieving early fame there: Haku, Barbarian and Earthquake were all sumo wrestlers, while the British Bulldog, along with his partner, Dynamite Kid, helped mold Nipponese tag team methods in the early 1980s.

As time passed, competition heated up between the WWF's finest superstars and standouts from the Land of the Rising Sun.

....

Fans go wild when WWF superstars visit the Land of the Rising Sun and go against top Japanese wrestlers.

Among others creating heart-stopping reactions in Asia were Hawk and Animal, the Legion of Doom. With their power moves, face paint and "take no prisoners" outlook, the LOD boasts a style never before encountered in Japan's rich wrestling history. Wherever they go in the country, they are mobbed by admirers and media representatives, but Hawk and Animal have made it clear that they don't journey across the time zone for fan veneration.

"We come here for the competition," Hawk told reporters during a 1991 tour. "The LOD bestows no praise on mortal peons, but the country of Japan has earned our respect. They take their wrestling seriously here. It's never 'just another match' to the Japanese wrestlers. We want 'em to come at us with their torpedoes blasting. When it's all over, the LOD will be standing over the smoldering ashes, while our opponents — whoever they may be — will be missing in action."

The words sounded typical of a wrestler in foreign territory, attempting to intimidate with brash boasts. But Hawk and Animal never speak without knowing that they can back up their words. Days after the interview, they plowed through Japan's best competitors to win the first-place trophy in the Super World Sports (SWS) — an Asian wrestling federation associated with the WWF — inaugural tag team championship. The LOD squared off against six opposing teams, finally downing the

competent squad of Tenryu and Hara in the final round.

What made the victory headline news in Japan was the fact that Tenryu — who teamed with former sumo star Kitao to best Demolition at *WrestleMania VII* — is considered one of the finest wrestlers the country has ever produced. For several years, he has had a respectfully competitive relationship with both the LOD and Hulk Hogan. In the name of sport, he has stood on the opposite side of the ring from the above-mentioned stars. But when situations have warranted, he has proudly joined their sides to achieve a mutual goal.

Aside from Tenryu, numerous other SWS stars have offered the WWF wrestlers powerful competition. These include Naoki Sano, a light-heavyweight partial to spectacular high-flying maneuvers, and Sato, an original member of Mr. Fuji's dreaded Orient Express.

Although many fans in Japan look at WWF visits to their country as clashes between Eastern and Western culture, the majority of the stars regard the tours differently. To them, the WWF represents not any particular country, but a strong commitment to excitement and fun on an international level. ■

WWF wrestlers are generally bigger than Japanese stars, who put great reliance on speed.

CATCH AS CATCH CAN

The story of the World Wrestling Federation is one of success. The WWF empire attracts eight million fans a year to live events, while its merchandise, television and other divisions flourish.

Along with rock star Cyndi Lauper, Hogan helped create the Rock 'n' Wrestling Connection, a movement matching the muscle of the squared circle with the thunderous sounds of rock 'n' roll.

The most visible figure in the WWF is, naturally, Hulk Hogan, who's engendered a worldwide movement known as *Hulkamania* and has charmed entertainment industry moguls and film buffs with the same adeptness he's used to overpower his dangerous opponents in the ring.

Hogan's dynamic energy was first spotted by Sylvester Stallone, who cast the bronze-skinned, golden-haired superhero as Thunderlips, the champion wrestler who almost dis-

The more Hogan accomplished in wrestling, the greater the demand for him was outside the ring. He appeared on numerous talk shows and specials — country singer Dolly Parton featured him in one of her videos — and spoke of one day making a film if the right kind of script came along.

His moment came in 1989 when he starred in *No Holds Barred*, a film made by Shane Productions, which has the same parent company as the World Wrestling Federation.

Hogan played Rip, a superhero whose family loyalty forces him into battle against one of the most dangerous men on the planet.

A devious television executive, Tom Brell (Kurt Fuller), is infuriated that he cannot entice Rip to do business with him. So Brell searches the depths of society until he finds Zeus (Tiny Lister), a phenomenally strong, maniacal ex-con, and gets him to physically conquer Rip. Rip ignores his adversaries' challenges until Zeus attacks the wrestler's brother. Then the two engage in a brutal no-holds-barred contest in a futuristic ring.

Oddly enough, the battle carried over away from the movie set. Apparently, Zeus thought that he was good enough to take on the Hulkster within the confines of the World Wrestling Federation. In several matchups with Zeus, Hogan proved to be the better man — both on the screen and in the squared circle.

Like the real-life Hogan, Rip is a wrestling champion and role model for millions of children who believe in his positive message.

mantles the Italian Stallion bone by bone in *Rocky III*.

At the time, many Hollywood insiders were saying that the Hulkster's future was on the silver screen. But first he had business to tend to between the ropes. He captured his first WWF Championship in 1984 and teamed with television star Mr. T in the main event of the inaugural *WrestleMania* in 1985.

Hulk Hogan has appeared with many other stars, including country singer Dolly Parton (*left above*). As Rip in the movie *No Holds Barred*, the Hulkster engaged in an epic battle with the monstrous Zeus, who later challenged him in the real WWF ring.

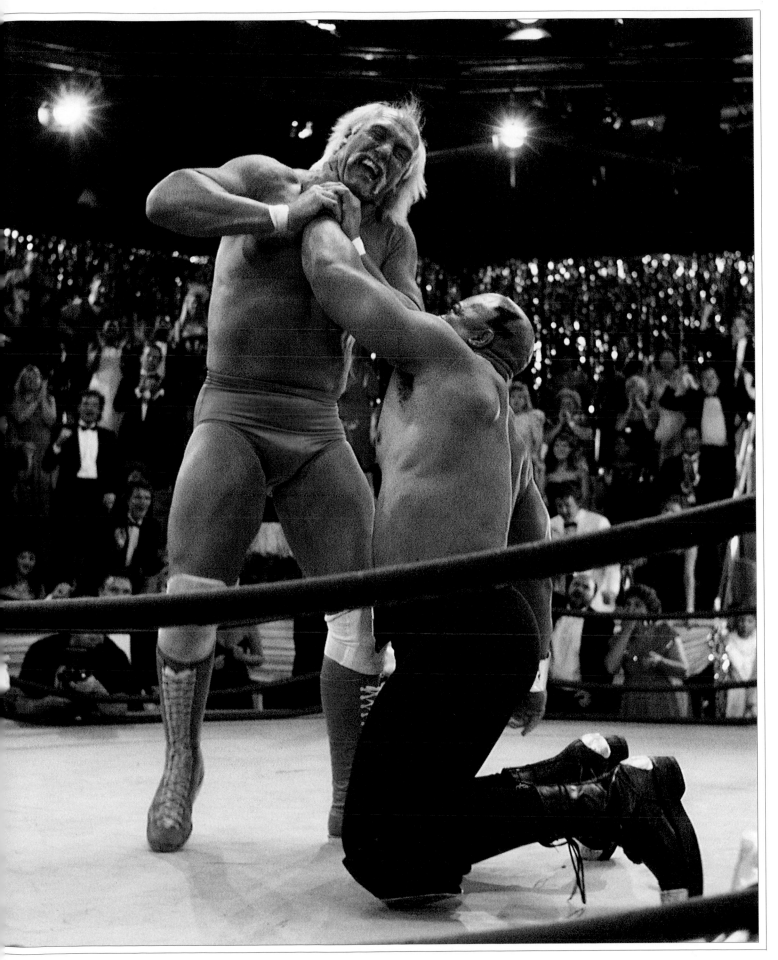

In his intergalactic combat gear, Shep, played by Hulk Hogan, is ready for the foul minions of General Suitor in *Suburban Commando*.

In 1991, another cinematic opportunity came the Hulkster's way. This time it was a starring role in *Suburban Commando*, the tale of a gladiator who comes from outer space and befriends an innocent family.

Hogan plays Shep Ramsey, an intergalactic warrior who accidentally ends up on Earth and moves in with Charlie and Jenny Wilcox, played by Christopher Lloyd and Shelley Duvall.

Mr. and Mrs. Wilcox, a good-natured couple living in a typical American community, aren't quite sure what to make of the muscular stranger who tells them that he's from France. But their children take an immediate liking to him, so the Wilcoxes figure that he can't be all that bad.

Then Shep's enemies from outer space, led by the sinister General Suitor — played by William Ball — show up for some high-tech battles, leaving the Wilcoxes wondering whether they would have been better off finding a mellower tenant.

Following the success of *No Holds Barred* — and unexpected fanfare

resulting from the Hogan-Zeus war — the Hulkster was offered a multitude of scripts to read, but he had something specific in mind. He liked the fact that *Suburban Commando* was an action film involving the development of a friendship between Shep and Charlie Wilcox, two individuals from literally different worlds.

The movie starts off with a bang in the first scene as Hogan, playing Shep, crashes his way through several decks of his enemy's space ship, blows open the bridge's doors, penetrates a force field and disposes of General Suitor's soldiers. But before Shep can take on his nemesis one-on-one, the General mutates himself into a vicious intergalactic monster, forcing the hero to retreat.

Knowing that he is being pursued by bounty hunters commissioned by Suitor, Shep sails through space. He meets an unexpected adversary, however, in the form of a comet storm that damages his ship and forces him to land on the nearest planet, Earth.

Trying to remain inconspicuous until he can resume his space feuds, Shep moves in with the Wilcox family and develops a sympathetic fondness for Charlie Wilcox, a nice guy who can't seem to get the recognition he deserves at work. It is Charlie who trails Shep to his hidden space ship and discovers his tenant's secret.

Shep becomes an inspiration to the hapless Charlie, who begins to borrow from the stranger's courage. When General Suitor's mercenaries find their way to Earth to face off against Shep in a tumultuous final confrontation, the luckless husband becomes the visitor's brave ally.

The types of thrills experienced by movie theater patrons watching *Suburban Commando* are felt weekly by fans enjoying WWF telecasts. ∎

Through his travels, Hogan had developed a special kinship with children and thus wanted to appear in a film targeted for the whole family.

Shep meets some of the kids in the neighborhood where he has sought shelter in *Suburban Commando*.

Rowdy Roddy Piper, Gorilla Monsoon, Mr. Perfect, Bobby "The Brain" Heenan and Vince McMahon carry on a lively discussion on WWF Television's *Prime Time Wrestling*.

The World Wrestling Federation Television Network is the largest syndicated network in the world. In North America, more than 300 stations show WWF broadcasts, making them available in 97 percent of the United States. Internationally, weekly

and *WWF Wrestling Spotlight* — regularly rank among the top five American shows in syndication.

The nationwide USA cable network also broadcasts *WWF Prime Time Wrestling* and *WWF All-American Wrestling*. Both of these shows rank

> **"** I'll go down as the greatest broadcast journalist of all time. **"**
>
> BOBBY "THE BRAIN" HEENAN

programs are taped in several languages — English, Spanish, French, Arabic and German — and distributed in more than 50 countries.

In Europe, the WWF is affiliated with broadcasting giants: British Sky Broadcasting in England and Ireland, Canal Plus in France and Editmedia in Spain.

The three programs syndicated in the United States — *WWF Superstars of Wrestling, WWF Wrestling Challenge*

among the three top regularly scheduled programs on the popular cable channel.

The format of *WWF Prime Time Wrestling* is particularly intriguing. Between matches broadcast from capacity-filled arenas, wrestling experts sit around a table and debate the merits and faults of the WWF superstars. On a typical program, it is not uncommon to see commentators Vince McMahon and Gorilla Monsoon arguing the strong points of fan favorites such as Hulk Hogan, the British Bulldog and Rowdy Roddy Piper, while on the opposite side of the table, Bobby "The Brain" Heenan and Mr. Perfect with the Reverend Slick hype the virtues of such questionable characters as Ric Flair and the Undertaker.

"From my exposure on *WWF Prime Time Wrestling*, I've come to be regarded as the foremost broadcast journalist in the United States," manager Bobby "The Brain" Heenan — better known as "The Weasel" to his detractors — pronounces immodestly. "I've been told that, in the United Kingdom, Robert Maxwell was planning to put me in charge of his media empire at the time of his death. He understood greatness."

Although Bobby Heenan's words can rarely be believed, he does make the program entertaining — reminding many of the humorous *Tuesday Titans* show also seen on the USA network at the time of the first *WrestleMania*. To longtime devotees of wrestling in the United States, *Tuesday Night Titans* provided some unforgettable moments, with its talk-show format, its endless array of guests and co-hosts Vince McMahon and Lord Alfred Hayes.

On the NBC television network, the WWF's Saturday Night's *Main Event* specials ran for several seasons, in place of the comedic *Saturday Night Live* — the show that spawned the careers of John Belushi, Chevy Chase, Eddie Murphy and others — often drawing higher ratings.

....

The Million Dollar Man Ted DiBiase exults after Andre the Giant beat Hulk Hogan for the title on *Saturday Night's Main Event*.

On Friday, February 5, 1988, television history was made in America with the airing of the WWF's *Main Event* on NBC, a one-hour, primetime special drawing a 15.2 overnight rating and 25 share. Translated into layman's terms, that means a national television viewership of more than 33 million followers — the largest audience ever for a WWF telecast.

Those who saw the program still speak vividly of the strange events that transpired that night. In a title match between World Wrestling Federation Champion Hulk Hogan and Andre the Giant, the referee registered a three-count on the Hulkster, even though his shoulder was clearly off the mat at the count of two. Things got weirder when the title belt was awarded to Andre and he quickly "surrendered" it to Million Dollar Man Ted DiBiase. Viewers soon learned that Hogan's loss was instigated by the scheduled referee's evil twin — who was on the Million Dollar Man's payroll — while the real official was tied up in the dressing room. After the match, WWF President Jack Tunney deemed the championship null and void and declared a tournament to determine a new kingpin. After a night of grueling clashes, Macho Man Randy Savage won the tournament at *WrestleMania IV*.

WrestleMania IV, like all of the *WrestleManias*, had a major impact on the burgeoning pay-per-view television industry in the United States. The technology, which allows each fan to pay a fee to unscramble a signal on the cable system, was first tried — more as an experiment than anything else — at *WrestleMania I* in 1985.

Approximately $300,000 was grossed, and the decision-makers at the WWF chose to pursue pay-per-view further.

Six years later, the results of their experiment had cable industry executives shaking their heads in absolute amazement: *WrestleMania VII* grossed $24 million.

"When we ran our first pay-per-view event in 1985, 17 cable systems offered it to a universe of 300,000 homes," recalls Richard K. Glover, who heads the WWF's pay-per-view activities. "*WrestleMania VII* was carried by 1,258 systems to a universe of 16.5 million homes."

The WWF presents four major pay-per-view specials each year: *WrestleMania* in the early spring, *SummerSlam* in late summer, *Survivor Series* in late November and the *Royal Rumble* in January. Additionally, there are other pay-per-view events throughout the year, such as *WrestleMania's History and Heroes*, a documentary of *WrestleMania* highlights, and *This Tuesday in Texas*, held on December 3, 1991, at the request of WWF President Jack Tunney, following the questionable circumstances surrounding Hulk's title loss to the Undertaker several days earlier. ∎

....

Hulk Hogan and Andre the Giant clash on the *Saturday Night's Main Event*. WWF superstars are seen on television worldwide.

In every city during the WWF's European tours, Make-a-Wish has arranged for chronically ill children to go backstage and meet their heroes.

· ·

Hulk enjoyed volunteering his time at the International Special Olympics in Minneapolis, Minnesota, in 1991.

Despite the level of attention thrust on the WWF superstars, they still find time to sneak away from the spotlight to bring joy to those less fortunate. WWF Charities is a little-publicized division of the World Wrestling Federation. Since late 1986, the WWF has been involved in programs designed to reduce drug abuse by young people. Between matches, the foremost personalities in wrestling have made stops at schools, hospitals and other facilities with a powerful but simple message: "Just say no."

Aside from his triumphs between the ropes, Hulk Hogan has evolved into one of the most beloved celebrities in the world, and he's taken great steps to live up to his reputation. Hogan is an honorary board member of the Starlight Foundation, an international organization that grants wishes both to terminally ill and to disabled children.

In both Europe and the United States, the WWF has worked closely with the Make-a-Wish Foundation, which does similar work. The WWF has also been involved with the American Cancer Society, Juvenile Diabetes Foundation, International Special Olympics and other groups.

The personal appearances only fuel the immense popularity of WWF merchandise. How popular are the dolls, T-shirts and drinking mugs depicting the titans of the mat wars? Industry sources estimate that WWF properties brought in about $1.7 billion in 1990. There are more than 400 products manufactured exclusively for the World Wrestling Federation, including WWF Action Figures and Toys; Wrestling Buddies, pillow-like figures of WWF superstars; trading cards; apparel; posters; WWF Superstars Ice Cream Bars; computer games; foam versions of the Big Boss Man's nightstick and Hacksaw Jim Duggan's two-by-four; Nintendo Video Games; Hulk Hogan Children's Vitamins; and WWF Cookies.

When people come to the arena to see the matches, they often return home with a souvenir or two. They also buy products through the official WWF merchandise catalog featured in WWF publications.

Additionally, over 100 WWF videocassettes, distributed by Coliseum Video, are available. To show the enormous appeal of *WrestleMania*, advance orders of the videos of *WrestleMania V*, *VI* and *VII* were platinum before they even hit the stores.

Seven cassettes have gone platinum, and three have gone gold.

Over the years, a number of the wrestlers have also tried their luck at singing — with surprisingly successful results. *The Wrestling Album*, released in November 1985 by CBS/Epic Records, caused shock waves in the music business by going

gold. A follow-up album, *Piledriver — The Wrestling Album II*, released in October 1987 by CBS/Epic, spent 20 straight weeks on the Billboard charts and went gold in Canada.

In the United Kingdom, *WWF Magazine* became the largest selling imported publication in the country, as the WWF superstars were touring Europe in 1991. Worldwide, the paid circulation is 400,000, but the readership is estimated to be something over two million.

WWF Magazine, the official publication of the WWF, is the only wrestling magazine taking fans right up to the WWF ring, where the wrestlers' bulging veins and red-faced grimaces are captured by official photographers, whose dramatic prints of life in the squared circle have appeared in *Sports Illustrated*, *Time*, *Newsweek* and other journals. The shutterbugs have also followed the titans on their days off as they relax at home, play at the beach, meet with fans or conspire against their rivals. From time to time,

WWF Magazine, the world's number 1 wrestling magazine, is the flagship of WWF Publications.

new occurrences in the WWF are scooped by *WWF Magazine* before television viewers receive the news.

Therefore, it is no surprise that, for the six-month period ending December 30, 1990, versus the same time frame in 1989, sales of the publication shot up 20 percent.

Other special WWF publications include *WWF Wrestling Spotlight*, a four-color quarterly exploring the career and personality of a WWF star such as Hulk Hogan, Rowdy Roddy Piper and Elizabeth; *WWF Superstars*, a vivid photo essay of the world's top wrestlers, in the ring and away from it; and *WWF Program*, a 16-page colorful publication sold in arenas and published monthly. Among the most cherished programs are those commemorating historic events such as *WrestleMania* or the *Royal Rumble*. ■

INDEX